Tales from the Locker Room
An Anecdotal Portrait of
George Szell and his
Cleveland Orchestra

Lawrence Angell
Bernette Jaffe

Tales from the Locker Room
An Anecdotal Portrait of
George Szell and his
Cleveland Orchestra

ISBN - 9781626130531
Amazon Edition

Published by ATBOSH Media ltd.
Cleveland, Ohio, USA

www.atbosh.com

Acknowledgments

Our most since thanks to all who participated in the interviews.

A special thank you to Dick Wright for drawing the caricatures and to the many musicians who loaned us photographs.

Introduction

In 1987, my husband, Sam, and I became snowbirds splitting our time between Cleveland and Sanibel, Florida. During our years in Cleveland, the orchestra and many of the musicians had become an important and rewarding part of our lives. Arriving in Sanibel, we found an enormous void, very little live classical music available and just a small "mom and pop" cultural organization known as "Big Arts." Gradually with the help of like-minded individuals, Big Arts expanded to include a few classical music offerings each year. The first group to perform was the outstanding Amici Quartet, all members of the Cleveland Orchestra. Also we thought it might be a good idea for Big Arts to showcase some student musicians so I called Linda Cerone at the Cleveland Institute of Music who graciously recommended a student violinist, She said that she would ask one of her most remarkable faculty members to accompany the violinist. "You will love her," Linda told me.

Several weeks later the day came. Anita Pontremoli and her husband, Lawrence Angell, arrived at Big Arts, she to rehearse and he to critique. In my mind, this love affair did not have an auspicious beginning. Anita and Larry arrived 45 minutes after the appointed time, delayed by a tennis game!

After brief introductions and some deep breathing on my part, I said to Larry: "I know you. You play bass in the Cleveland Orchestra." He assured me that was so but that he had retired five years earlier. I insisted that could not be true because I still saw him there on stage!

Needless to say, he cut an important figure. It wasn't long after that first meeting that I learned he loved to regale us with orchestra stories, and trust me, there was always a story. And, of course, Linda Cerone was absolutely correct. Anita and I became inseparable friends.

One day I suggested to Larry that he should write down some of the wonderful anecdotes and tales that he loved to tell so they would not be lost to future generations. We began to expand on this idea and thought there might be several musicians who had played in Szell's orchestra who would be eager to participate in this project.

I took part in all the interviews but Larry did most of the interviewing. All the interviews were tapes (those tapes are available) and it was my task to transcribe them and consolidate them into a hopefully readable and engaging book that provides insight into the times, the conductor and the players who made this orchestra great.

Bernette Jaffe

Preface
Lawrence Angell , Double Bass, 1955-1995

In the late seventies at intermission of a Maazel rehearsal Bill Kiraly, seated at a table in the locker room, beckoned to me: "Larry, I've got something that might interest you." Bill was a violist with many interests- especially a keen interest in baroque music. He held up a copy of the current Early Music Journal for me to see and opened it to an article about the annual Lord Mayor's concert of London. The year was 1700 and there was a reproduction of the actual front cover page of the program. "Turn the page," he said, "and look at the personnel list." When I got to the names of the double bassists, there it was, a Mr. Angell! "Now turn to the next page," said my friend. Again there was another program of the Lord Mayor's concert. The year was 1725 and there he was, Mr. Angell again, still playing bass for the Lord Mayor. Had I been a bassist, this bassist, for all this time?

My fifteen years with George Szell left an indelible imprint. I still feel Szell's eyes looking over my shoulder, guiding my musical thoughts and, through me, those of my students. I began writing this book because I knew I was not alone with these memories. So I sought out veterans of that era to tell their tales of how George Szell created an orchestra like no other. He remains for many in the musical world a giant whose intellect and aristocratic taste have yet to be duplicated.

He was a man of contrasts. He could make decisions with laser-like clarity, evaluate players who would best contribute to his orchestra, lead 100 individuals and mold them into a chamber music-like

3

ensemble.   He could interpret the intentions of a composer without sentimentality.   Even the most familiar music was fresh and inspired.

We, the players, were Szell's tools to attain his musical vision. He was demanding, sometimes cruel and intimidating, always sure of his goals and how to achieve them.   Many of us reacted with resentment to his controlling demands; others accepted the pressure without protest.

Through the eyes of these artists I want to preserve the individual memories and impressions not only of the man who was George Szell but of the atmosphere in which this great orchestra flourished. It was thus that I interviewed many of my colleagues, some by phone, some face to face, some individually, some in groups — but all the musicians interviewed worked directly with Szell. Many of them had been refugees from Western Europe and the Nazi terror. Szell was able to draw upon the European musical traditions and American technical skills and combine this mix to create an orchestra that played with artistic depth, verve and brilliance, ever striving to reveal the essence of the composer's intent.

In Szell's day, the conductor reigned supreme. He hired and fired, dictated dress code and discipline. The musician's union did not nurture the welfare of the players. Despite poor remuneration and conditions, the players persevered. There were so many unique, lovable characters in this orchestra. It is to them that I dedicate this work with gratitude. And especially to my friend and colleague, Marc Lifschey, whom I single out because he played such a prominent role in the memories of many of Szell's musicians. He was one of those rare individuals who changed my life forever. And the sound that came from his oboe was often a miracle; so miraculous it astounded his colleagues.

In the following pages you will find Marc's name mentioned often as colleagues attest to the complex relationship Marc had with Szell. I think Szell was harsher with Marc than with any other player because he understood Marc's extraordinary gifts.

Just when I was about to graduate from the Eastman School of Music I heard about an unbelievable opportunity...a double bass position had opened in the Cleveland Orchestra! I remembered when the Orchestra was playing at the Community Concert Series in my home town. I was a junior in high school and playing in a great orchestra was only a fantasy to me. I found out where the orchestra members were staying and went to that hotel in hope of catching a glimpse of "real" symphonic musicians. By luck, I arrived just as they did and saw the typical confusion — people checking in and bustling about. But something seemed odd: the hotel lobby was very big but all the musicians were standing lined up against the walls. Nobody ventured into the middle of the room.

I stood in the center of the lobby but soon felt a strange sensation at my back. As I turned I looked straight into a gray wool overcoat. As my eyes continued to the head above, I realized I was being confronted by a very tall man wearing glasses thick as milk bottle ends. His magnified eyes glared at me as if to say: what is this...this...creature? There I was...eyeball to eyeball with George Szell. Suddenly I understood why the players had crushed themselves up against the walls. Among those musicians waiting to check in to their rooms would have

5

been legendary harpist Alice Chalifoux, 'cellists Martin Simon and Robert Ripley, violinist Kurt Loebel, assistant conductor Louis Lane, piccolist William Hebert, bassoonist George Goslee, and oboist Robert Zupnick, all dedicated, energetic, each in his or her own way helping Szell to create an orchestra "Second to None." I was fortunate to have the opportunity to interview these players almost 60 years later!

Alice Chalifoux, Harpist, 1931-1974

A rookie musician soon learned he was in the company of a rare personality when encountering Alice, the orchestra's harpist for 43 years. I asked her if she was the first woman to join the orchestra. "I think there was a viola player," she said. "We used to call her 'Olive Oil' after that comic strip character. I forget her real name."

Alice, a sweet, charming Southern girl, grew up in a convent school in Birmingham, Alabama where she began her harp studies. In her late teens she auditioned for the distinguished harp teacher, Carlos Salzedo and was accepted at the Curtis Institute of Music in Philadelphia. She became a member of the Cleveland Orchestra in 1931 and also became one of the busiest harp teachers in America.

She learned quickly, through necessity, how to get along with her male colleagues. Dressing room accommodations for women on tour were rare or nonexistent so she changed clothes inside her harp trunk. Her banter and colorful vocabulary — for a protected southern girl — allowed her to be "one of the boys" and get along hilariously with all her colleagues.

Alice was hired "way back yonder" by Nikolai Sokoloff (the Cleveland Orchestra's founding music director) and played under Artur Rodzinski (1933-1943) and Erich Leinsdorf (1943-1945). "Then Shtikfort showed up. That's what I called him sometimes. I don't know how you'll put that in your book."

"What precisely does Shtikfort mean?" I asked trying to keep a straight face.

"I think it's a Yiddish word. I got it from one of the orchestra members. Most of my material came from the 'boys'. You'll have to figure it out for yourself."

I asked Alice what George Szell was like when she first met him. She said she couldn't remember but was quick to add that he didn't change over the years. "He was a great teacher. Who was that Frenchman who used to play with us? He was a pianist."

"Casadesus?"

"Yes, at rehearsals they were both trying to give the orchestra lessons and trying to outtalk each other. It was very funny and we all sat there deadpan."

Alice recalled a conductor who was always trying to get out of conducting but realized it was not Szell. "Szell," she said, "would conduct if he were on his last legs. As a matter of fact, he was and he did. We got off the plane from the Japan tour and he went right to the hospital and died two weeks later."

Alice then reminded me how Szell loved to give Clifford Curzon lessons when he came to give a guest performance. One day, in exasperation, Curzon slammed down the lid of the piano and said, according to Alice: "Get someone else to play your damn concerto" and then stomped off the stage. Then there was a lot of shouting backstage and everyone crept off the stage and went home.

I asked Alice if she remembered an episode with Heifetz. She digressed to tell me that Mrs. Heifetz (Frances) used to live next door to her in Birmingham. "Frances always liked fiddle players so she married one. She went right to the top." I reminded Alice of the "episode" when, during a storm there was a startling noise above the stage. Szell ran off but no one else moved including Mr. Heifetz. When Szell finally reappeared outside his dressing room Frances gave him hell and told him he was a coward.

Alice described the time she was backstage with Mr. Szell waiting to go on stage as the soloist. "I asked Mr. Szell: 'Does this ever get easier?' He responded: 'No, Alice, but some people mind more than others.' Alice didn't think it was difficult for Szell except for the time when the orchestra was playing in upstate New York and Szell's first wife was in the audience. "I think Joe Gingold (the concertmaster) told us it was his first wife. Szell was a mess. He was shaking. Usually he never batted an eye."

Lisa Wellbaum, formerly Alice's student and principal harpist of the orchestra from 1974 to 2007 quoted Alice that Szell looked like he was "goosing butterflies" when he conducted. Lisa recalled that Alice took eight of her Cleveland Institute of Music students to Dayton for a harp ensemble performance and assured the dean beforehand: "Don't worry. They're all virgins."

Quips like these led Johnny Carson to invite her as a guest on his "Tonight Show" television program.

I reminded her that the last time I saw her was at the Cleveland airport. She was traveling alone for a weekend in London. I teasingly suggested that she must be off to see some man, to which she replied: "I always knew harpists. Those tours were fun."

Alice was 97 at the time of this interview.

Louis Lane, Conductor, 1947-1974

I sat in Louis' living room with his grand piano and a spectacular view of Lake Erie and downtown Cleveland. Louis had given much thought to the experiences he wished to share with me. It was 1947 and he was completing his studies in composition and piano at Eastman when he read an announcement on the Conservatory bulletin board. Szell, the newly appointed conductor of the Cleveland Orchestra was hiring two apprentices. "I hadn't been invited anywhere to write the great American symphony. I had studied composition with Bernard Rogers." I interjected: "Good man," to which Louis replied: "For those who liked him, yes."

Louis hadn't thought of being a conductor and the job requirements didn't say anything about conducting. "They specified a pianist of professional capabilities (which, for me, was a stretch), somebody who could sight read music, transpose and read a score and indicated a hearing test with unspecified details. The candidate would conduct the first movement of a symphony either by Brahms, Beethoven or Mozart, singing, humming, or whistling the leading voice. There would be no orchestra and no actuality of an orchestra but you were to act like you were conducting the orchestra.

"So I applied and to my amazement received a letter inviting me to audition at ten o'clock in the morning about six weeks away. I started looking at the Brahms symphonies and decided they were all too difficult for me to conduct. Then I started with number nine of Beethoven and worked backwards. I hesitated over number one thinking perhaps I could do it but then I read Nickolai Malko's "Conducting Manual" and decided it was too difficult. Then I started on Mozart 41, 40, 39 on down and finally got to 28. That I thought I could do. So I memorized it on the train from Rochester to Cleveland and wrote it out on a piece of paper. I knew it reasonably well.

"I arrived at Severance Hall in good time and told Clyde, the doorman, that I had an appointment to see Mr. Szell at ten. He told me he couldn't take me up before ten because 'Mr. Szell has a way of using all his time.' So exactly at ten, Clyde knocked on Mr. Szell's door. When he opened it I said: 'I'm Louis Lane.' He said: 'I'm pleased to meet you. I understand you are from Texas.' 'Yes, that's true,' I replied. 'Well,' he said, 'I've never been to Texas except driving across the northern panhandle once and that wasn't very appealing.'

"He asked me to play the Brahms C major Sonata and half way through the development section of the first movement he said: 'I think that will be enough. I can see that you play the piano reasonably well. I don't know that I would call it exactly professionally well but it is on the borderline.' Next he handed me the Chopin E major Etude and said: 'I'm sure you know this piece.' I replied that I had never studied it but had played it through for myself. He said: 'Play it for me in D flat.'"

That was a heart stopping request but Louis played it very carefully and got through a couple of pages when Szell stopped him and said: "You have made two mistakes. Do you know where they are?" Louis did know and pointed them out. Then Szell pulled out a gigantic volume without showing Louis the front page. He opened it to a page he had marked and said: "Do you have any idea who wrote this?" Louis studied it intently and said: "The only composers who probably could have written it were either Wagner or Bruckner because they are the only ones I know who use horns and four or five Wagner tubas." Szell finally identified it as the third act of Gotterdamerrung and asked Louis to play it. When he finished Szell said: "That's not how I would have done it but you didn't make any errors."

After putting Louis through hoops a few more times they at last got to the symphony he had chosen. "My, what an odd choice," said Szell. "I hope you brought a score because I don't know it." Louis had a miniature score in his pocket and gave it to him. "Szell started humming it so I began conducting and after a while he stopped me, saying: 'You just sang the first oboe part in this last bar. What is the second playing in that bar?' My mind went completely blank. Then it occurred to me that maybe there wasn't any so I said: 'I don't believe the second oboe plays in that bar.' 'Quite right,' he said, 'carry on.'" When Louis came near finishing the piece, Szell was still not quite satisfied and gave him the Beethoven Sonata, Opus 54 to orchestrate as far as he could go in exactly one hour. "So in exactly one hour he returned, looked at what I had done and said: 'That's plausible, that's the style, that's even charming. I think you will do'"

Seymour Lipkin, the other apprentice and a brilliant pianist, was Louis' mentor his first year. "I was in so far over my head that I really didn't know what was going on. I would whisper to Seymour: 'Why did he stop?' to which he would reply: 'Because.' Seymour was used to people with big egos.

Since the apprenticeships were to last only one year, Louis prepared for an audition at Rutgers. The morning he was to leave he was summoned to Szell's office. "He told me then that he had been disappointed with the quality of those who had been auditioning for the apprenticeship for the following year. 'You haven't done badly this year. How would you like to come back?'" So began a tenure that lasted an additional twenty-three years.

Once when the orchestra was returning by train from a successful concert in New York, Szell asked Louis to suggest some shorter pieces that the orchestra might play. He told Louis: "Next year in New York there will be the most saintly of seasons." "Saintly?" Louis asked; "Yes," he said, "saintly." "Well," said Louis, "that's remarkable. I never heard of building a program around saints." "Yes," he said, "the whole season will be saintly and I'll show you why." So Szell got out a pad of paper and showed Louis three of them: St-okowkski, St-einberg and St-ravinsky. **Our three saintly conductors.**

Szell liked to cook and I thought that Louis might have experienced his cooking. "Occasionally he invited me to his house on Friday afternoons to help organize his library. We would work until early evening when Mrs. Szell would often invite me to stay for dinner. One of these times Mrs. Szell was outside digging in her tulip garden when Szell decided to go to the kitchen and correct her stew. 'She never puts in the right ingredients and spices.' After a while, we heard a loud voice exclaim: **'George, what have you done to my stew?'**

"Once I was at their apartment for dinner after which we sat in the living room and Szell said: 'I need a few more overtures for next season.' I said I had an idea so I went to the piano and played the beginning of a piece. Szell was visibly upset and yelled: 'Stop, stop. I won't have that trash in my program.' Mrs. Szell piped in

14

and said: 'Why, George, I thought that was rather nice.' 'Well, it isn't nice,' he replied. 'But do you remember the second theme?' I replied that it was a sort of inversion of the first theme only in B flat. 'Yes,' he said. Mrs. Szell asked him why he hated it so much. So I answered that it was Mr. Szell's composition "Lyric Overture," Opus 5. She snapped back: 'Where did you find that trash?' I told them I had discovered it in the Eastman Library. I thought it was ingenious and reminded me of Strauss's methods of procedure. 'Well, you have said it,' he responded. 'That's just why I stopped composing.'"

I asked Louis how Szell sought out and trained musicians. In response he quoted Szell's reply when asked that in the Soviet Union: "First rhythm, second, rhythm, and third, a sense of tempo. After that: technical ability, tone quality, a good ear, and the ability to listen and play at the same time."

Louis admitted that there were many times Szell was very difficult. "After the principal horn had a bad time one year on tour, Szell called in Angelucci (third horn who could do no wrong in Szell's eyes) and told him he would like to appoint him first horn. Angelucci said: 'Thank you very much, Mr. Szell, but I cannot accept the position. I'm a little too comfortable in my lifestyle and I don't want to be on pins and needles all the time.'"

Louis recalled that Rafael Druian, who replaced Joe Gingold as concertmaster, alienated most of the players during his nine-year tenure. He lacked the tact and diplomacy necessary for his leadership role. I asked Louis about Druian's sudden departure from the orchestra. "There was a recording session on Monday morning. However, Columbia Records, by mistake, had shipped their equipment to St. Louis instead of Cleveland

15

so the session was delayed until Tuesday. Saturday night prior to the recording session, Trogden, the personnel manager, went around and told everybody but he forgot to tell Druian because Druian didn't speak to Trog either.

"Monday morning came. Druian showed up for the recording session and seeing no one on stage figured that there must have been a cancellation. He went upstairs, pounded on Barksdale's (general manager) desk and told him what an incompetent he was and how miserably the orchestra was run. He wanted Mr. Szell to call him personally and apologize. With that he left and Barksdale went down to tell Mr. Szell.

"I was called to Szell's office immediately. There was Barksdale, one cigarette on the corner of the desk, lit, another cigarette on the other corner of the desk, lit, and Barksdale lighting a third. Mr. Szell said: 'Lane, what would you do?' I said: 'It is not proper for you to ask me that question and it is not proper for me to answer it. However, I have a question for you. What have you been training Daniel Majeske for over the past ten or twelve years?'

'Oh,' he said, 'what an interesting thought you put in my mind.'

George Carmer was to be Szell's spokesperson if Druian called or came in. But Druian didn't phone and didn't show up. When he didn't show up for the Thursday morning rehearsal, Szell said: 'That's the end. He has violated his contract and I will speak with Danny at intermission. The announcement will be made tomorrow.'"

16

Robert Ripley, Cello, 1942-1943; 1946-1955

Bob joined the orchestra in 1942 in the Rodzinski era but was there only two weeks when he was called into service. He returned in Szell's first year, spent nine years with him and "learned a lot. It was nine years of the greatest conservatory anybody could go to. He was a born teacher. It was his whole life and he expected that of us."

Bob described Szell as infinitely patient with some players but unwilling to give artistic freedom to others. "It was one of his flaws. He wanted everything to be perfect according to his standards. I remember one huge blowup. When we had finished playing the Brahms Violin Concerto with the beautiful oboe part in the slow movement, Marc (Lifschey) made a gesture with his hand saying: fuck you. Szell was furious. The anger carried over to the next night when we were rehearsing the choral movement of the Beethoven Ninth. Szell started slapping on his stand and shouting at the orchestra: "I'll teach you to play in rhythm, god dammit."

Bob played with Charles Munch in Boston. "It never occurred to Munch to rehearse in minute detail, but that was Szell's whole shtick to a fault. We recorded the Eroica with Munch and I compared the two 'Eroicas,' Szell's and Munch's. Despite often complaining about Munch, I liked his sense of free feeling in the recording better than Szell's perfection." That was the common criticism. Szell believed in micro-management, micro-conducting and micro-rehearsing. Once he said: "Now, gentlemen, we will rehearse the spontaneity." It was meant to be a joke!

Bob described Szell as a metronome with soloists. We did the Tchaikovsky with Milstein. In rehearsal Szell was not pleased with Milstein's rhythm. He said: "Look, I have a metronome in my heart and you are rushing." Once when Szell was playing and conducting a Mozart piano concerto he was so uptight. He had endless rehearsals and in the final rehearsal he told the players: "If I go ahead you simply have to go with me."

"Occasionally in rehearsals Szell tried to be funny. Once he came dashing on stage, which was not his style, climbed on the podium and said: 'Let's plunge into the Bartered Bride.' No one reacted so he said: 'Did I say something funny?' Embarrassing.

"Then there was the momentous time when the Cleveland Indians won the American League pennant. Before the rehearsal the musicians spread the word to start with something appropriate to celebrate. So when Szell gave the downbeat for the Berlioz Overture, the orchestra started playing 'Take Me Out to the Ballgame.' Though he claimed to know every piece of music, **that** he didn't know and, puzzled, turned to Gingold who told him what it was and why we were playing it. 'Oh, I see,' he said, 'well, come on.' We began our normal rehearsal."

Robert Zupnick, Oboe, 1946-1977
Martin Simon, Cello, 1947-1995
Kurt Loebel, Violin, 1947-1997
Donald White, Cello, 1957-1996

Bob: It was difficult to see the human side but there was a soft side. I sound empathetic. Many people had bad thoughts of him but we are indebted to him for being an outstanding conductor and teacher. We got famous by riding on his coattails.

Larry: You said it so well. We are recording now.

Bob: Oh, my god. I could write this book.

Larry: So you could. What was it like when you first played an audition?

Bob: Actually I didn't have an audition. I had just finished four years in the army and bumped into Harry Fuchs, a fine cellist in the orchestra, who told me: 'We have a guest conductor named George Szell (who at that time was conducting at the Met).' So I called and made an appointment to play for him. I was given fifteen minutes during which I played half a dozen excerpts from memory of some compositions that featured the oboe. The last piece I played was the opening passage from 'Le Tombeau de Couperin' by....

Marty: Ravel

Bob: That's right, Marty. Szell made one small correction. Otherwise he didn't stop me. He thanked me and I left. Six months later the general manager called to say that Mr. Szell was going to be the Cleveland Orchestra's new conductor. He intended to enlarge the size of the orchestra and asked me to be assistant principal. Growing up in Cleveland, the Cleveland Orchestra was my standard, my idol, the orchestra I looked up to like kids looked up to Babe Ruth or Lou Gehrig if they liked baseball.

Larry: I remember a time when Marc Lifschey took ill just before a concert at Carnegie Hall. The Brahms Violin Concerto with its famous oboe solo was scheduled. Do you recall that?

Bob: No, but I must have blocked it out. Elden Gatwood reminded me of that occasion once and said: "You know you played beautifully."

Larry: With no rehearsal — at Carnegie Hall!!!

Bob: There were those moments. Marc was a marvelous oboist but his attendance record was a bit questionable. Many times I played on short notice — it took all the fun out of it.

Larry: I would say so. Marty, do you recall your audition?

Marty: First I must say that Bob is far too modest. In 1965 he saved the Russian tour. That was a big tour and Bob was in his room day and night making reeds. If he had not been there it would have been a disaster. The first oboist had problems with the conductor and had to leave and Bob was the replacement. It was drastic and dramatic.

Bob: I was definitely on the hot seat.

Larry: Do you remember frigid winter tours, when we would take the Pullmans out of New York to Elmira or Wilkes Barre or some god-awful place, sometimes bumping into Szell on the street? The elevator was a particularly bad moment.

Bob: One week when Rudolph Serkin *(pictured)* was soloist playing a Mozart concerto, I played principal oboe. The following week we were on tour. The first stop was Syracuse and as I was walking through the lobby of the Hotel Syracuse, Mr. Szell approached me and handed me a small package. "This is for last week," he said. It was a lovely necktie.

Larry: Really!!

Bob: And once Mr. Szell called me into his office and gave me a box of Whitman's chocolates. He had a human side.

Marty: I remember some of his more sarcastic remarks. I think it was a William Schumann piece, perhaps "New

England Tryptich." We were rehearsing for Oberlin. Someone asked: "Which Schumann are we doing, the New England piece?" Szell responded: "No, Schumann — the composer."

Bob: Early on Szell was unhappy with the Saturday performances. He believed the quality was below the Thursday night performances and he threatened to have rehearsals on Saturday mornings. Immediately the situation improved.

Larry: Did you feel some fear during your time in the orchestra?

Bob: That was standard. You got used to it. Larry, when we started this conversation you asked how we feel now. I can't believe how I did it. My first concert with Szell was October 1946. I came when he first started. We played a Brahms symphony and he rehearsed it with a fine-toothed comb. The concert went so well and I thought that we would never be able to do that again but every week was with a fine-toothed comb and every week the quality stayed up. Of course, you remember Moe Sharp. He finished playing a solo passage, turned to me and quietly said: "I'll never be able to do it that well again." He was pulling my leg.

Larry: Moe said if he knew he was going to live so long he would have taken better care of himself.

Bob: You would see him on tour in some restaurant with a martini in one hand, a cigarette in the other and a smile on his face.

Larry: He could play fabulously even with one or two martinis before concerts. It never showed. Marty, you had some run-ins with Szell surely.

Marty: He did have a sense of humor. He told me once: "Why don't you play pianissimo. If one can't hear you, it can't be wrong." A little biting.

Larry: He was good at that. I am told he said to the double basses (before my time in the orchestra): "Why don't you play it as if it were a **musical** instrument?" Or the time he asked a violinist: "Did your teacher ever give you lessons in rhythm?" Knowing he was in a no-win situation, the violinist replied: "Yes, sir, of course he did." Szell said: "Tell him to give you your money back."

Bob: When George Millrood fell on top of his violin and smashed it into a thousand pieces, he went to tell Szell and all Szell could say was: "Don't you have another?"

Marty: I remember a story about how John Browning, on the Russian tour, got up his courage and asked Mr. Szell: "How did you get to be that good?" to which Szell answered: "I'm not that good. The others are that bad."

Bob: Somebody once said about Szell that if he had been a German general during World War II we would have lost the war.

Larry: What about the way we dressed on tours?

Marty: We were in shirts, ties, hats — no beards.

Bob: Lenny Samuels grew his beard after Szell died — a symbol of liberation and defiance. The administration tried to ban it and when they didn't succeed, they instituted a series of fines. Lenny never would shave so they finally gave up.

Don: Once in Lucerne when von Karajan was conducting, Szell sent word that he wanted to see me. Since I didn't play the first number, I got to the hall late and was immediately told by some of the guys that Szell was looking for me. So I was shaking in my boots. He found me at intermission and said he wanted me to play for him when we got back to Cleveland. That ruined my whole trip. However, upon our return, there was a strike for three days. When I asked if he still wanted me to play for him, he said: "NO!" Later he moved me up in the cello section. I thanked him. "Do you want to play for me now?" he asked to which I responded: "No, thanks."

Larry: After a concert in Santa Fe we were waiting to take a train across the mountains to California. I was always enthralled by trains and I began to talk to several of my colleagues about the romance of railroading as I pointed out the two or three Diesels that were going to pull us over the mountains. As I spoke I soon became aware that my colleagues were looking past me and there was Szell listening to the whole thing. I thought: oh, god, he is going to correct me or criticize me. Instead he just walked off into the semi-darkness toward the locomotives, eyed them up and down and started climbing a ladder on one side of the Diesel to peer into the engineer's cab. When he was part way up a guy with a striped locomotive engineer's hat appeared and said:

24

"Hey, you. What the hell do you think you're doing there? Get off my train." Szell said: "I'm the conductor of the Cleveland Orchestra" to which the man replied: "And I'm the conductor of this train. Get your ass off my train, **now!**"

Bob: Similarly, we were on a bus on tour when Mr. Szell stood up while the bus was in motion. The bus driver ordered him to sit down. Szell replied: "I'm George Szell, the conductor of this orchestra." The bus driver shouted back: "Sit down. I don't care if you are Lawrence Welk."

Kurt: I'll tell you how it all began for me. When I told people I was going to work for Szell, they said: "Oh, my god," so I got early warning signals. I auditioned for Szell in New York and he offered me the job. I was married just a few months and asked to discuss it with my wife. He said: "Mr. Loebel, take it or leave it," so I thought I should take it. He continued: "See Mr. Vosburgh over there and sign the contract." I started to read the contract and Szell said: "Never mind reading it, just sign it." I walked out of the room in a state of shock. I figured if I lasted a year it would be a miracle. At the outset, Szell told me: "Mr. Loebel, I don't like the way you do business."

Larry: How did you feel at your first rehearsal when the orchestra began to play?

Don: I was dumbfounded. I couldn't move. My hands didn't move. I was looking at the players and thinking: I've never been in an orchestra like this.

Kurt: You asked earlier if there were any incidents that occurred with soloists. I recall Erica Morini playing the Mendelssohn Concerto. During the rehearsal, Szell said to her in German: "You play like a pig, a swine." She said aloud: "Someone defend me."

Marty: I think it was more like "I won't let you get away with this." She was a wonderful fiddler.

Don: Marc Lifschey played the oboe solo in the Brahms Violin Concerto, the slow movement. He was slower than the soloist. Szell tried to tell him that he had to play faster but he didn't. Finally Szell stopped conducting and just let him play.

Larry: Szell had a strange relationship with Marc. He wanted to be his father but Marc already had a difficult father and mother. Szell knew Marc was extraordinary, probably the finest oboist anywhere, but he could not bring himself to praise him. Instead he used harsh criticism and intimidation. Marc told me: "He said I played like a gypsy whore."

Bob: He couldn't live with him or without him. Once in rehearsal he told Marc: "You sound like an oboe player from the provinces of Italy."

Larry: Jacques Posell was leaving the hall one evening and ran into a bit of bad luck. He met Szell who was coming out of his studio. Apparently things had not gone well with the bass section at that day's rehearsal. Szell confronted him: "What the hell has gone wrong with the damn basses? They're bowing every which way. It's chaotic." Jacques, almost tongue-tied, reflexively responded: "Well, Mr. Szell, down bow, up bow, how wrong can you get?" Szell was so shocked that anyone could think in those terms that he just let it go. He had no answer.

Did anyone here ever ask Szell for a raise?

Kurt: I did. My mother was very ill and I really needed a raise but when I approached him, he said: "We are prepared to lose ten people but any time you want to, you can come and cry on my shoulder." It's just the time in one's life when one wants that kind of answer.

Larry: The best one I heard about raises was the one about Abe Skernick. Everyone knows that story. Abe's wife was pregnant.

Marty: Oh, that one!

Larry: I guess I shouldn't tell it.

Marty: You can tell it.

Larry: They were starting a family and Abe knew he would need more money. The manager had no permission to do anything so he knew he had to ask Mr. Szell.

Kurt: The manager was busy carrying Szell's briefcase.

Larry: Szell grumbled about the raise but did give it to Abe. Another year or two at the most, Abe came back to Szell and said: "I've got to have more money. My wife is pregnant again." The third time he came back Szell lost his patience and said: "Abe, for god's sake, haven't you ever heard of fucking for fun?"

Bob: One time when he was the soloist, Nathan Milstein came on stage looking very debonair, hair slicked down and very self-confident. He had a cigarette holder sticking out of his mouth and started rehearsing. While he was playing, Szell reached over and took the cigarette out of his mouth.

Don: I remember a story about Rafael Druian.

Bob: He passed away.

Marty: Everyone passes away sooner or later.

Martin Simon, Cello, 1947-1995

I had an opportunity to speak with Marty on a second occasion. I knew that Marty had grown up in Berlin and thought he might have attended the Hochschule fur Musik but he corrected me. He explained that during the Hitler years he was not allowed to go to the Hochschule. He left Germany when he was seventeen and went to study with Silva in Italy.

"Luigi Silva?" I asked. "He came to Eastman at the end of his career."

Marty informed me that Silva had taught at Eastman but mainly at the Mannes School. "So you were seventeen when you left Berlin and then?" Marty, in his elegant, soft-spoken manner proceeded to tell me what had happened.

"We went to France, a long story. It is a story of the one who got away. And so did my parents, barely. And my sister and brother-in-law. They got papers from Joan (wife of violinist Felix) Freilich's father who was in children's apparel on Seventh Avenue. He signed one hundred affidavits of support to get people out of Germany. I actually studied with Silva in Venice.

"Really," I said still a bit confused, "and then you studied with Silva later at Mannes?"

"No, I studied one year with Silva and that was in Venice. I really didn't have enough time with him. I left Germany in 1938 just before Kristallnacht. While still in Germany, I studied with Ernst Silberstein who was in the famous Klinger Quartet. Klinger had taught Suzuki who came to Berlin to study violin about 1910."

I told Marty that I often wondered how he and so many others in our orchestra were able to live through such horror and move on with their lives. He could only solemnly reply that "many of us came with long stories." But, in my humble opinion, it was those who came with their long and difficult histories who brought so much color and soul to the orchestra. This gave Szell some extraordinary musicians with whom to work, many interesting characters who brought their personalities and hearts to music making. I asked Marty what it was like working with Szell. He believed that, for the most part, Szell ignored him but occasionally directed nasty remarks to the cello section as a whole. He was a hard taskmaster and difficult. I then told Marty that I had read a biography of Feuermann. Feuermann was close to Szell and died at a young age in 1942. Marty reminded me that Szell gave the funeral speech and so many of the greats of the music world were there.

From my reading of the book I recalled that as young men starting their careers, both Szell and Feuermann played in small towns around central Europe. At one such town Szell had been appointed music director of an orchestra and along came Feuermann who had a concert in that same town. Everyone showed up early in those days unlike today. He came a week early just to get adjusted to the water and the locale. As he got off the train with his cello, he saw a big poster advertising the coming symphony season and announcing the news of the new music director, George Szell. Feuermann knew that Szell was a bit of a stick in the mud but that he loved to play chamber music. So Feuermann took a marking pen and added a note to the poster announcing that in addition to the regular concerts there would be an "elaborate chamber music season featuring George Szell as pianist." So many people believed it was true that a

Laszlo
Kraus

puzzled Szell had to play two or three chamber concerts because of demand.

Marty recalled hearing Szell play the piano with Ernst Silberstein, the A major, the third Beethoven sonata, with one rehearsal. "Szell was fabulous," Marty told me, "and Ernst was Ernst." I couldn't help but interject that we always wondered how Ernst got the job. We thought Ernst had something on Szell from the days in Berlin! I asked Marty if he remembered Laszlo Kraus.

"Yes," he said with a sparkle in his eyes, "Szell used to say Laszlo was illiterate in seven languages. That was Szell, too. He had a hard time with Laszlo because Kraus was an artist, always painting and sketching. Szell asked him: 'When do you practice?' to which he replied: 'I don't practice. I take naps.' Szell pursued him: 'Why do you paint?' 'Because I like painting. I don't like practicing!'

"Laszlo, Joe Gingold and I were among the twenty who came in 1947. When Szell came in 1946 he replaced several people with displaced Europeans and some Americans. Gingold wanted to be welcoming to Laszlo and invited him to his house to play string quartets. Laszlo thought a minute in his seven illiterate languages and said: 'I don't give a play very many but since you asking I'm doing the best that I are.' I still remember that from 1947. He also used to say: 'How did you came? Did you flew?'"

Wanting to tap into Marty's own facility with languages I decided to remind him that Alice was always calling Szell "shtikforts." "Do you know the translation of that word?"

"That was her name for Szell. She would say to Otis, the doorman: 'Has old shtikforts come in yet?' He would reply: 'No, Miss Chalifoux, Mr. Szell has not come in.'"

We then reminisced about what made Szell different as a musician. "I loved the way he made music," said Marty. "I listened to the 'Schubert C major' the other day — a forty year old recording and it was fabulous. It couldn't have been better."

As we talked about Szell being letter perfect I remembered another conductor who was also letter perfect. One time Szell was rehearsing the NBC, Toscanini's orchestra, in the "Eroica," dissecting it note by note, stopping every three or four measures and making the players resent him terribly, muttering to themselves: you're trying to teach us the "Eroica" liked we've never played it before? Some time before intermission there was a noise in the hall that turned into a kind of roar. Toscanini came running down the aisle shouting at Szell: "How dare you try to teach my orchestra how to play the 'Eroica.' You'll never conduct **my** orchestra again, **ever!**"

I asked Marty what he knew about Szell's accepting a position teaching theory at the Mannes School when he first came to America. At that time conducting opportunities were few and far between. "It was great," Marty said with a small smile. "He wasn't teaching. He was showing off all the time, sitting at the piano and playing everything from memory. He played all the Beethoven Quartets on the piano and he was terrific."

We then discussed how Szell related to the musicians in a personal way. The public seemed well aware of his tyrannical leadership. What they didn't see was an occasional soft spot when he would send flowers to the hospital or offer more time off following the death of a family member. I asked Marty what he remembered about Szell and Lynn Harrell. "He gave Lynn lessons forever," he said. "Lynn told Harry Fuchs that he hit him and Harry asked: 'Why didn't you hit him back?'"

"He hit **Lynn?**" I was astounded.

Allen Kofsky, Trombone, 1961-2000
William Hebert, Piccolo, 1947-1988
George Goslee, Bassoon, 1943-1945; 1946-1988
Gino Raffaelli, Violin, 1957-2000

Bill: It was 1947, my first year in the orchestra. Szell had scheduled the Tchaikovsky Fourth Symphony with its difficult piccolo part. I made the entrance on this solo one bar too soon and knew Szell would call me in so I decided to preempt him and speak to him immediately: "Mr. Szell, I feel terrible I laid such an egg," I said to which he replied: "Yes, that was a very nutritious one. It should last you for a long time."

Gino: At my audition Joe Gingold was on stage assisting in the slow movement of the Mozart E flat Symphony. Szell called out from the audience: "Ask him to use our fingerings that are written in the part." I did but didn't play very well and Szell asked a surprised Joe to show me how it should be played.

Initially I was terrified coming into the orchestra but I soon came to admire Szell's interpretations and his ability to control the orchestra. Without doubt, he was the greatest conductor I had played with but at the time I wasn't sure it was worth it. No conductor asked so much of the string section in terms of ensemble work and no one else could get that kind of precision. It was difficult then but now I am very proud to have been a part of it.

George: He was a musical giant. The four Schumann symphonies are probably THE best performances ever recorded. When Ivan Fischer conducted the orchestra he asked to speak to a few Szell era players to inquire about his rehearsal techniques and how he got such precision. Fischer said he liked to conduct the Cleveland Orchestra because it still played in the George Szell style. That irked Dohnanyi who didn't like our orchestra being called "George Szell's orchestra." But that was a fact of life.

Allen: Szell would often begin the first rehearsal of a new program of music saying: "Gentlemen, the Cleveland Orchestra starts rehearsing where other orchestras leave off."

The Moscow Philharmonic was on tour playing in Cleveland and the management brought them to hear an orchestra rehearsal at Severance Hall. Szell called an intermission but we didn't know why. Soon the orchestra's librarian came on stage and handed out the music to Strauss' tone poem "Don Juan," one of our signature pieces. We played it for them without a run through and they were stunned.

Szell was always concerned about our diets and would lecture us to stay out of "questionable joints." Once on tour in Worcester, Massachusetts I was out walking and bumped into Szell who asked why I was out so late. I explained that I was looking for hot chocolate. He approved because he thought hot milk was good for us. Nine years later we returned to Worcester and Szell asked: "Are you going out for hot chocolate after the concert?" Now Maazel had a photographic memory. Szell did not. He learned things by hard work. He really studied the scores but he never forgot **anything**.

Just before leaving on tour to Michigan, my third child was born. The bris (ritual circumcision on the eighth day) was to be the same day as our final concert in

Toledo. I asked Szell if I could fly home after the Thursday night concert, attend my son's bris, and drive to Toledo the next day in time for the concert. He flipped, he blew his top, he called in Beverly Barksdale and started pounding and said: "You will not be the first or last father not to be at his son's circumcision. If I hear that you left, I don't care if you come back. You are taking a chance." So I didn't go. We were able to make an exception and reschedule the bris for Monday.

Gino: In 1965 I was hospitalized with stomach ulcers the night before we were to leave on the Russian tour. A week later I was better and notified Szell that I would join the orchestra. Soon I got word from him saying no matter how soon I returned it would not be soon enough.

George: It was in 1968 at the opening rehearsal of the season. I had two Heckel bassoons but I hadn't used one of them and decided to try it. At intermission Szell called me into his office and said: "You don't sound the same." Sheepishly I told him I was using a different bassoon. He told me not to do that. So the next day I went back to the old bassoon and had a short solo after which he looked over at me and smiled.

Bill: When John Rautenberg first came to the orchestra he brought with him an old German wooden piccolo with a silver head joint. Szell wanted all wood, no silver. It was too brilliant. Szell had scheduled the "Dance of the Spirits" that calls for two piccolos and told John who was playing second to be sure to play down. At the concert he signaled Rautenberg to keep the sound down and he continued to do that every night. Finally John put black shoe polish on the silver and Szell said: "Much better."

Larry: On the Russian tour in Tiblisi, Georgia we were performing the "Daphnis and Chloe Suite No. 2" when the lights went out but the musicians continued to play from memory and finished the piece as the lights came on. The audience went wild. We played four encores. Later we performed in Sochi, a resort city on the Black Sea. Just before we started to play there was a tremendous disruption. People were shouting and scuffling to get into the hall if only to stand and listen. The concert was sold out. The townspeople tried to break down the doors to get in. We were so appreciated and respected. That tour was one of the highlights of my career.

Elden Gatwood, Oboe, 1953-1963

Szell telegraphed Marc Lifschey from Europe and asked him to find a second oboe player. As Elden described it: "I went up to a seedy hotel in midtown Manhattan and knocked on the door of Marc's room. He opened the door in his shorts, having just gotten out of bed. The shades were drawn and the room was dreary. I played for him, and after a while, he told me the position was mine. I was shocked because I had auditioned for about twelve orchestras and hadn't gotten a job yet!"

Surprised that Szell trusted Marc to hire someone, I mentioned this to Elden who assured me that "Marc knew a bit more about the oboe than Szell." Szell seemed to like Elden because he called him "Gat." Most players were referred to as second this or third that. But every time Elden heard "Gat" he shivered. He knew what was coming.

Szell often asked Elden to play louder and Marc insisted that he play softer. What a dilemma for Elden who finally learned somehow to compromise. I suggested that he was sitting in a danger zone right next to Lifschey. Elden acknowledged that Marc's behavior occasionally created difficulties and told me he received a telegram the day Marc was "fired" offering him a job. He was in the Pittsburgh Symphony as principal oboist at the time. He still has the telegram, which said: "Are you available and interested in the principal job in the Cleveland Orchestra?" Of course, Elden was very flattered but decided against accepting the job. First of all, he didn't have the nerves to play first oboe with Szell "who was so picky and heard everything anybody played" and secondly, he didn't want to follow a talent like Marc.

He was happy in Pittsburgh and found Steinberg to be a mensch, musical and relaxed and a person who fit Elden's personality better.

An oboist once asked me what it was really like when Lifschey was principal oboe. I asked him to imagine a theater marquee that said:

Marc Lifschey
and
The Cleveland Orchestra
George Szell, Conductor

Szell confessed his biggest mistake with the orchestra was letting Marc go. He told a local doctor/violinist: "This is the end of great music making in Cleveland."

Elden exclaimed: "Marc was **the** superb artist. I have never heard such a musical line. I knew I couldn't play in the same league with him. When I got the telegram about the principal job, I called Marc. It was the same afternoon of the day he had been "fired" and he didn't even know he had been fired. He told me he had just walked out of rehearsal because Szell said something about his pitch. He asked me not to do anything about the telegram until he got in touch with me. So I waited two or three days and felt I had to let Szell know. I was so frightened to talk to him and decided to give him an alternative name, Jimmy Caldwell, a fabulous oboe player. Szell apparently tried to connect with him unsuccessfully.

Elden recalled that one of Szell's favorite Haydn symphonies was number 88. "In the slow movement there is a little bird call in the second oboe. He bugged the crap out of me until I got the shortness he wanted and did this at each rehearsal." The orchestra did a runout to Lakewood and played the piece. The next morning before rehearsal, Szell came over to him and said: "What the hell were you doing last night?" all because Elden's instinct was to play it musically rather than the way he wanted.

"There was another episode I won't forget," Elden told me. "We all felt fear and terror despite the fact that it impacted the percussion section directly." Elden described it as the 'Bartok Concerto for Orchestra Episode.' Matson said every time we did that piece he had to see his shrink. Playing the very soft drum part that opens the fourth movement was excruciatingly painful for him. Szell knew what he wanted to hear but had trouble conveying it. It was never short enough or soft enough. Szell got perturbed with Matson and replaced him with Bob Pangborn but he couldn't satisfy Szell either. So Szell turned to tympanist Cloyd Duff. Cloyd repeatedly told him: "I am not doing it" and Szell replied: "You are." Cloyd told him: "You have ruined the best percussion section in the country." But Szell insisted and finally Cloyd said: "I'll play it on one condition, that you don't say a word to me about it."

Elden told me: "I will never forget this as long as I live. We played it next in New Haven. It was so fantastic. When we came to that movement Cloyd got up from the tympani and crossed the back of the stage to the percussion instruments. Our hearts were in our mouths. **Bam. Bam-Bam-Bam Bam-Bam-Bam-Bam Bam-Bam-Bam!** Cloyd struck the drum as long and loud as he possibly could."

I, too, couldn't forget that episode. Cloyd played in an angry, brutal way showing his fury with Szell. One could sense the whole orchestra slipping down in their chairs because the whole world was about to explode before their eyes.

Lawrence Angell, Double Bass, 1955-1995

I was in a room with a few other people, warming up, getting ready for the audition. A violist was there with his wife who kept going in and out of the room. Finally he was called to play and soon came back dejected. The audition had not gone well. He was obviously heartbroken. His wife started screaming at him: "You played like an idiot! How many times have I told you to stop this nonsense? You should just forget about this crazy music stuff." They didn't seem to notice me. But it didn't help ease my tension.

Eventually I was called to play. I was shown to the violin side of the stage. The auditorium was dark, the stage was brilliantly lit. I couldn't see anyone in the hall but someone had to be there. Finally someone asked me to play.

Because of short notice I hadn't worked up a proper solo or concerto. All I had prepared was the Mozart, K 612, a concert aria for bass-baritone with orchestra and double bass obligato, "Per Questa Bella Mano." The bass line is flashy and difficult and I was playing it as a solo without accompaniment — no orchestra, no pianist and no singer.

I realized this was about the most peculiar thing one could do at an audition — play obligato to nothing. I was sure I would make a thousand mistakes. After several minutes someone signaled me to stop... I caught a glimpse of bottle ends and a dry, kind of croaking voice asked: "Mr. Angell, just how many aw—chestras are there in Rawchester?" As I began a seemingly endless litany of the many student and professional orchestras in that musical city, it occurred to me that he knew exactly

42

the answer to his question. Suddenly interrupting, my interrogator said: "Oh, I see, Mr. Angell — so Mr. L-e-i-n-s-d-o-r-f conducts the 'shtudent' orchestra — Isn't that right?" Peeling laughter in the darkened hall was my first indication of the presence of an audition committee. My trial by fire was over. I was offered a position in this great orchestra. My professional life would now begin.

In the following pages I interview several of the players who joined the orchestra at about the same time as I.

George Hambrecht, Flute, 1955-1961

George's audition was "a very pleasant experience." He was in New York when a friend told him Szell was holding auditions in the city for the assistant principal flute position in Cleveland. George decided to audition and prepared important flute solos. At the audition he was asked to sight read some of the Bartok Concerto for Orchestra with which he was not familiar. In the small flute solo that goes up to high C, George didn't quite make it. However, Szell gave him a second chance and he got the job.

Of his first rehearsal George said: "I couldn't believe I was there. Wonderful music was happening and it was all I could do to keep up." During his first year, Moe Sharp "who hadn't missed a rehearsal or concert in twenty years" had appendicitis and George was called to replace him on first flute. Szell thanked him for an excellent job.

The Cleveland Orchestra during Szell's tenure became a unique ensemble. George described his experience akin to "sitting in the middle of a Swiss watch." During a performance of Mozart's "Jupiter" Symphony he realized "it was so incredibly perfect, the tempo, the musicianship, that the hair stood up on the back of my neck. Szell brought perfection to his job. I don't believe there's been anyone before or since who has been able to consistently give the definitive performance."

George's impression of Szell, the man, was somewhat different from mine. He remembered him as "wonderful to work for" but acknowledged that some people felt he was irascible and difficult. I remember his occasional cruelty to orchestra members and the heavy weight of his intimidation. George, on the other hand, recalled that "Szell never berated anyone on stage. If somebody made a mistake, he wouldn't glare at them. He would look the other way because he knew if he stared them down they would make another mistake. If a mistake was made, Szell handled it in private." I couldn't help but remind George that by the end of Szell's first six seasons he had created an astonishing number of personnel changes (Donald Rosenberg, "The Cleveland Orchestra Story," 2000, p. 253).

We reminisced about the great wind section in George's day. "Szell was there most of the time. There were very few guest conductors. Szell really led and shaped the orchestra. My eyes were on him ninety-five percent of the time. I was always watching him in case he wanted to double or to increase or decrease the sound. That happened occasionally but most of the time most of it was already marked in the score."

Hambrecht recalled that great artists loved playing with the orchestra, among them Rubinstein. "Everybody in the world was devoted to Rubinstein and Szell was completely blown away by his playing." George remembers Szell saying: "The art of playing in an orchestra is the art of accompanying."

Touring - Carnegie Hall

Touring, Szell knew, was essential to change a fine second level American orchestra to an orchestra "second to none" as he had promised its powerful board of trustees when he accepted the music directorship of Cleveland's orchestra. So it was that he chose to tour the northeastern United States in February, placing the all-important Carnegie Hall performances at the very heart of the concert season. The winter weather was daunting and would challenge us moving from city to city, but no matter. With some luck and his willpower we would be there with the downbeat on time. In fact, February's weather also worked in favor of touring because many of the orchestra's important patrons and trustees were customarily in Florida choosing to avoid Cleveland's winter woes.

At any rate, program planning, scheduling, and performances were all aimed at coming to a frothy perfection for the eastern tour. All concerts in all cities were important but some performances seemed to serve as open rehearsals for the concerts in New York. Szell would conduct looking for trouble. Perfection had better be there even if inspiration was lacking.

We came to New York prepared to make music like no other orchestra, to be recognized as the **"Rolls Royce of Orchestras."** In time, critics and audiences came to realize that concerts by the Cleveland were unique. American precision that combined European artistry, aristocratic taste, perfectly balanced ensemble, became the hallmark of this great orchestra. Its music was satisfying to the mind and heart.

Anshel Brushilow, Violin, 1955-1959

Anshel and I began our careers in Cleveland at the same time but he left in 1959 to become concertmaster of the Philadelphia Orchestra. Speaking with him by phone, he sounded exactly as he did back then. In Cleveland he was assistant concertmaster and sat with Joe Gingold for four years. "We became like brothers," he told me. "During recording sessions, while Szell listened to the playbacks, we played poker." "Ah, yes," I said, "you were in the high-low game with David Arben and Ernie Angelucci."

Anshel remembered a particular recording session when the orchestra had returned from break and began to record again. "I started to laugh hysterically. Joe looked at me like I was crazy and pointed to the microphones but I couldn't stop. Finally I whispered to Joe: 'His fly is open.' 'Oh, my god,' said Joe, '**You** tell him.' '**Me?**...**You** tell him.' 'All right,' said Joe. So he got Szell's attention, picked up the music, stepped the two or three feet to the podium and, pretending to discuss a fine point in the violin section, said: 'Your fly is open.' Szell quickly turned around, zipped his pants, and went on."

Anshel told me another story, this time about Vronsky and Babin, the husband/wife piano team. "I used to giggle a lot and when I started to laugh, Joe would start to laugh also. If I laughed hard enough, I had tears in my eyes and couldn't see the music. Victor wrote a concerto for two pianos for himself and Vitya. The concerto had a very tough orchestral entrance after the cadenza in the first movement. To find that entrance Szell would start to conduct early. We had the bar numbers in the part. He would conduct the cadenza so we would know where we were and he would know where to give the cues to come in. I said to Joe: 'I think he is going to have problems.' 'Don't be silly,' said Joe. 'He's conducted this kind of thing before.' Thursday night we all managed to get through it. At Saturday's performance during the cadenza he looked like he was erasing a blackboard. I started to laugh and Joe started to giggle. Then we began to laugh very hard. Szell had his head in the score trying to figure it out and he stopped conducting. Chet Roberts, the tuba player, decided he knew where we were and started to play. Then Marcellus started and the rest of us started. I looked over at Victor Babin and he was looking at us as if to say: have you lost your minds? Szell was waving his hands madly. There was so much chaos that when I turned a page Joe looked at me and said: 'What are you doing? I'm still on the other page!' Finally the movement ended."

Anshel's mention of Chet Roberts reminded me of the time when the orchestra was recording a Wagner album involving a lot of brass. Sometimes when something wouldn't go right, Chester would say in his radio voice: "Maestro, perhaps it would go better on the contra B flat tuba that I have in my garage." Buying time he would come back with a different instrument for the next rehearsal. That worked well for him but once when we were recording Szell worked on a certain tuba passage that didn't satisfy him. He was always deferential to Chester. They went over it again and again. Finally Szell said: "Should we do it one more time?" Chester replied: "No, Maestro, I think I should quit while I am ahead," to which Szell replied: **"What makes you think you are ahead?"**

Thinking of Chester reminds me of a story that circulated about his efforts to get a raise. One such time he was so frustrated that he mustered up all his courage and dignity, banged his hand on Szell's desk and said: "If I don't get this raise right now, **I Resign**." Szell banged his hand on the desk and said: "**I Accept!**"

I asked Anshel to tell me a story he had alluded to earlier in our conversation. It was on the 1957 European tour on a train in Poland. In some of the compartments there were three bunks, upper, middle and lower. Assigned to this particular compartment were Alfred Zetzer in the bottom bunk, Bob Marcellus in the middle bunk and Ernie Angelucci on the top bunk. Anshel describes it: "I don't know if you ever saw Alfred without a shirt but he was all hair, his whole back. He looked like a gorilla. The three of them went to sleep. During the night Alfred felt claustrophobic and decided he couldn't sleep in his bunk, so he took his mattress which was very thin and with his pillow put it on the floor of the train and lay down. After a while in complete darkness Angelucci decided to go to the bathroom so he jumped down, landed on Alfred and thought he had landed on an animal. He started to scream. Bob Marcellus, hearing the screaming, jumped up and hit his head on the bunk above. The three of them were screaming. Angelucci said: 'I thought there was some kind of dead animal on the floor.' And poor Alfred, it knocked the breath out of him. He couldn't do anything but roll from side to side."

Anshel had a good relationship with Szell who tended to take great talents under his wing and nurture them with a strange combination of cruelty and kindness. But I did recall a time Anshel was about to break a chair over Szell's head. "Yeah, that you remember," said Anshel and went on to elaborate two upsetting instances. The first was after he had played the Tchaikovsky during the summer program with Louis Lane conducting. Anshel asked that they make certain cuts made standard by Milstein known as the "Milstein" cuts. Louis agreed. "The next year Milstein came to play the Tchaikovsky with the orchestra, Szell conducting. During rehearsal Szell said: 'I found something in the score that I cannot believe. How could anyone make cuts like these?' "He ranted on, all the time knowing it was I because I'm sure he had talked to Louis. Finally he called an intermission. I stood by the podium and said: 'Dr. Szell, I could punch you right in the nose.' Joe said frantically: 'Anshel, let's go.' I refused and said to Szell: 'You knew I made those cuts and changed the bass line.' He stepped off the podium, put his arm around me and said: 'I love it when you're angry with me.'"

I found that response somewhat odd and encouraged Anshel to tell the second story. "It was the end of '57 and I was having lunch with Szell in Detroit where we were on tour. He said he knew he would lose me some day but, in the meantime, he insisted that I sign a three-year contract. Under pressure, I did. Almost the end of that season I got a call from Ormandy offering me concertmaster of the Philadelphia Orchestra. I said: 'You bet.' He asked if I could get free and I told him that I thought Szell would let me go. So Ormandy said: 'Let me know.' Unbeknownst to me, immediately following our conversation, Ormandy went back for the second half of his rehearsal and announced to his orchestra that the new concertmaster would be Anshel Brushilow. Jake Krachmalnick, the then Philadelphia concertmaster, was on stage and almost had hemorrhoids. That was the first he knew that he was to be replaced. Jake and Szell were very close. Jake got on the phone almost immediately and told Szell what happened. I went to work the next morning feeling terrific and knocked on Szell's door. After the third knock, the door flew open and Szell said: 'You are not going anywhere. I'm not letting you out of your contract.' He slammed the door in my face. I'm thinking how did he know? I was madder than hell so I called Ormandy who asked if I could shorten my contract to one more year and he would wait for me. So the next day after rehearsal I went back to Szell and asked Beverly Barksdale, the general manager, to be there. I requested that he shorten my contract by two years and he said: 'No, I don't want you to go. That's not the right place for you and you don't want to go.' He tried to persuade me but I insisted that I was going, and then he said something that got me very mad so I stood up quickly which frightened him and he ran behind his chaise.

"I said: 'I'm not going to hit you.' Beverly was sitting there saying: 'Can't we talk this out like gentlemen?' Finally Szell agreed to change the contract to one more year, which was fine with me and Ormandy. But the Philadelphia was going to Europe that summer and Ormandy asked me to join them, which I wanted to do. So I went to see Szell again and told him I was offered a summer job and suggested that we had nothing scheduled. 'Yes, we do,' said Szell. 'We're playing in Philadelphia at Robin Hood Dell while the Philadelphia Orchestra is away.' He wouldn't let me go.

"There was another incident that happened at the beginning of my second year in Cleveland. I arrived at the hall and went directly to Joe's dressing room. Excitedly Joe told me that the 'old man' wanted to see me right away. He had a surprise for me. Sure enough Szell told me that he decided to make me associate concertmaster instead of assistant. Stupidly I asked if there were more money involved. He slammed the desk and exclaimed: 'What's money? Money means nothing. It's the opportunity and the honor to be associate concertmaster and he lectured me. So I thanked him and went back to Joe's dressing room. 'Did he tell you?' Joe asked. I said: 'Yeah, you know, Joe, when you come right down to it, in abbreviation I'm still an ASS. Joe didn't get it: ASS-ociate, ASS-istant."

Touring Europe – 1957

The enthusiastic praise of the most important critics and the loyal allegiance of sophisticated music lovers was not quite enough to elevate the Cleveland Orchestra to the highest rungs on the musical ladder in the minds of the public, most especially at home in Cleveland.

Thus Szell decided it was time to compare these dedicated musicians to the very best in the music capitols of Europe. In 1957 the orchestra embarked on its first European tour visiting London, Paris, Amsterdam and Berlin among others. It was the tour that put the Cleveland Orchestra on the global map. In Vienna, hours before the concert, the leading music critic scoffed...Imagine those Americans coming to the city of **Beethoven**, playing his music for US...and coming from a city known only for its **Indians!** Imagine the orchestra's pleasure reading the superlative reviews following these concerts. We were being discovered.

Following are interviews of several players who were part of the orchestra that made this trip so monumental.

Warren Downs, Cello, 1956-1971

Warren was playing with the St. Louis Symphony when he heard about an opening in Cleveland. He auditioned and thought it went well "because Szell wasn't there at first. Abe Skernick and Joe Gingold were there and Szell came in when I was about a quarter of the way through the Haydn Concerto. At that point I stopped playing and tried to calm down a bit before playing for Szell." Moments later Szell called him in and invited him to join the orchestra. "I wanted to think about it and call my wife and Szell said I must let him know that day." So he accepted and was able to go on the European tour in 1957.

Warren found Szell easy to work with at least in comparison to his former boss, Vladimir Golschmann, whom he described as a "very emotional, scatterbrained Frenchman who played a lot of French music. His rehearsals were chaotic. He would stop the orchestra saying: '**No, No, No, No**' and the orchestra knew he was letting off steam. We all kept on playing. It was relaxed but tiring. Then when I came to Szell's rehearsals they were so efficient, so disciplined. I didn't think he was tyrannical in general although sometimes he picked on people.

"When things went wrong in the first violins, Gingold interceded between the section and Szell by turning around to them and saying: 'Have a look at that, gentlemen, have a look.' He was a wonderful person.

Phillip Naegele, Violin, 1956-1964

The following is a letter sent to me by Philipp Naegele who was a long time professor at Smith College. He was involved in Marlboro and the Music from Marlboro series. In lieu of an interview he chose to write down some of his thoughts about the Szell years:

In the winter of 1955-1956 I was on tour as concertmaster of the Seventh Army Symphony and first violinist of its String Quartet.... Years earlier my Viennese violin teacher in New York had said to me, apropos of future work, that if I wanted to play in an orchestra where my orchestral experience would be of the highest artistic quality, the only place to go was to George Szell and the Cleveland Orchestra. So I wrote Szell a letter, long hand, explaining my musical and academic mixed background, my teacher's advice, and my association with Adolf Busch and Rudolph Serkin at Marlboro...

Almost by return mail there came a letter in forceful fountain pen handwriting from Szell suggesting a meeting and audition with him in Salzburg in spring, there being two violin openings in the orchestra. Some weeks passed and we happened to be playing in Bavaria just before the appointed time to go to Salzburg, right close by, and a weekend pass was granted to me as well as to my stand partner, Leonard Felberg, who took off for Amsterdam to audition for the Konzertgebouw!

In Salzburg I went to the Mozarteum in uniform with fiddle. There was George Szell at work with the Vienna Philharmonic. After first thinking I wanted to be a conducting intern — heaven forbid — he told me to warm up in his dressing room and await his return from the rehearsal. I was practicing the Beethoven concerto when the door opened and Paul Doktor (son of the violist of the old Busch Quartet) looked in to ask what I was doing in Salzburg. On hearing my ambitions he laughed and asked whether I was ready with "Don Juan." I told him that in the Seventh Army we could do Brahms and Sibelius, but Strauss was out and I had never played "Don Juan." He made an unforgettable face and wished me good luck against all odds. Then the door opened and Szell came in. He asked me what I was going to play and proceeded to change his shirt while I got through the opening octaves of the Beethoven and the exposition. Then he asked me whether I had brought my Strauss excerpts...I explained...he made a face and said he usually gives "Don Juan"...(At that point I did not know yet that, when faced with the same piece to read, Berl Senofsky replied: "Are you kidding?"). Then he sent for the Vienna Philharmonic's librarian and told him to bring whatever was in the first violin folder. He came back with a very thick folder containing two Mozart symphonies and a Mozart piano concerto that Szell was to play. I sailed through the trickier stretches and was relieved to hear him say: "I'll take a chance on you. The management will send you a contract." I asked: "First or second..." "First!"

Meanwhile back at the Seventh Army Symphony, Leonard Felberg and I greeted each other with relief and delight not to have to commiserate or dissemble. I promptly applied for an early discharge, tried to get in some kind of shape and appeared at the opening of season rehearsal only to be confronted by "La Valse," a sea of sound in which I swam, hoping not to show my lack of experience in such repertoire, or make a false move and earn one of Szell's searching looks for the culprit. My seat, outside seventh stand in the firsts, seemed right under Szell's nose. But the first experience of the Cleveland orchestral sound was both exhilarating and sobering — how to be worthy of such quality and of such seriousness of intent on everyone's part, such symphonic chamber music!

Recordings of Strauss and Wagner that first season, of all things! I finally got my chance to learn "Don Juan" for real. My teacher had been so right about the orchestra and Szell. My eight seasons were a defining time in my professional life, shaping in serious ways everything that followed when I finally left to teach at Smith College and pursue chamber music. When I told Szell about my plans he said I would probably be back in Cleveland after a year at Smith. (I still went on the European tour in 1965 having been away all season — just in time to witness the Lifschey debacle that deprived us of his playing on the eve of leaving for Russia.) The orchestra had played at Smith College in Northampton, Massachusetts for many years, including my eight. Szell loved to play there before a devoted audience. Monica Feuermann, the cellist's daughter, went there. She arranged for us to show a Feuermann film in the music department. A good many players came as did Szell. There was Monica, a lovely undergraduate, playing her tragically and prematurely deceased father's performance of the Dvorak Rondo, with Szell in tears. Hardly the only human moment in my experience of Szell — his empathy when my mother died and my son was born; his faithfulness toward older European emigre players (Gans, Antal, Krausz, Silberstein) for whom there would have been inadequate retirement, but most of all his uncompromising artistic seriousness.

That seriousness was not fully appreciated by many in the orchestra who found it rigid, intimidating, unspontaneous, and over-controlled. That Szell came from a school devoted to the majesty of the score, to the realization through the orchestra of the integrity of chamber music — all that was not as well understood then as it came to be in retrospect. Now the Szell years count as a golden age. Then they were compromised by struggles with the management and the union over contract ratification, over security, indeed, over a living wage! The $7000 yearly minimum seemed to us in the rank and file the goal of our efforts in 1960! There was ... much discontent... all explainable, perhaps, on economic and psychological grounds but an unfortunate part of American orchestral life. The orchestra as a social and artistic entity seemed to me potentially the ideal community...I tried to hang on to that perspective then as I do now but it never seems to get easier. When we were suing for contract ratification and I said something about the "double minimum" that the union and management had once instituted, Szell told me ...he didn't like the company I was keeping (meaning the activists in the ranks)...

I give Szell great respect for his support of Robert Shaw...Think of James Levine as a conducting fellow then! ...Imagine American musical life without the special profile of the Cleveland Orchestra!

David Arben, Violin, 1955-1959

"Every morning I look in the mirror. I see **him!** He lives here and I don't know him. Dangerfield said: 'If you are a bisexual you have a fifty percent better chance to get a date on Saturday night.' People like this die. So many schmucks are alive. I was wracking my brains about George Szell and there is nothing I can come up with."

What a beginning to my interview and so in keeping with David's personality. I reminded him about the time he played the Mendelssohn Concerto with the Cleveland Orchestra on a Sunday, Bob Shaw conducting. His response was: "That was a long time ago. It's forgotten." I pressed him further, knowing full well it was not forgotten. I asked him what Szell said to him at the intermission of that concert.

"What did he say?" David repeated. "Nothing. I don't know whether he was stupid or trying to be nice, maybe both." So I asked him again what he said. "He said: 'Arben, your musical taste is impeccable.' But, see, the thing is..." I interrupted him and told him that Szell said his musicianship was impeccable!

David took a deep breath and went on. "The thing is that when I left for the Philadelphia Orchestra and tried to make a brochure, I wrote to Szell asking if I could use that quote. He sent me a letter on Cleveland Orchestra stationery, a printed letter, no signature. It said: 'George Szell' but no signature. He said: 'I'm sure, Arben,' (he never called me David or Mr.) 'you will understand that I am reluctant to put something in quotes I have said some time ago. Good luck.'"

So I then assured David that he had come up with a great story.

"I'm glad you like it," David replied. I explained to David that we do not have to use his name with any of the stories but if Szell told me my musicianship was impeccable ...at which point he quickly interrupted me: "look, did I say I was miserable?"

I asked David if he remembered any special incidents that occurred with soloists. He recalled a time at rehearsal when Clifford Curzon was the soloist. Szell moved Curzon aside from the piano bench, sat down and showed him how to play a passage. Curzon, about six feet four inches tall, rose to his full height and said: "You don't need me," and walked off stage. Of course, he came back.

I then remembered a time when Curzon was coming on stage to play his first rehearsal and Szell said: "Well, now that Clifford is Sir Clifford and has been knighted by the queen, it will be interesting to see how this has improved his musicianship."

"Yeah, nice man, full of compliments," said David. "I think it was when Heifetz came to play the Brahms Concerto, there was a phenomenal storm during the rehearsal which caused some debris to fall from above the stage. Heifetz didn't move. He stood with his violin in his arms, turned his head and watched Szell run off stage.

I remembered the incident very clearly, especially when Szell yelled: "Run, Marc!" (to Marc Lifschey) and left the rest of us on stage. Marc was so embarrassed and didn't know what to do. Szell wanted to save Marc and didn't give a damn about Heifetz or any of the rest of us. David reminisced about what a great player Marc was. "I haven't heard such playing since and I probably never will."

David was a member of the Detroit Symphony when he came to audition for the Cleveland. "It was not like today," he said. "It was George Szell and Joe Gingold. I played Bruch and 'Don Juan' but just for a short time and they offered me the job. In those days the conductor had all the authority."

I asked David about his first rehearsal with Cleveland. He described the process in those days. Officially, he was sitting in the last stand of the first violins next to Ed Matey but frequently he was moved from stand to stand. In this way he learned a lot quickly from the savvy and experienced musicians of the first violin section. I reminded him how Ed used to tap young musicians on the head with his bow when they were about to make a mistaken entrance. "He was absolutely terrific," said David. "Today new young players are pushed in the back and they all think they are great. They insist on not playing together. Not only do they insist but they succeed in not playing together."

David described what it was like to ask Szell for a raise: "You went to the horse's mouth. It was the end of my first season. He said: 'Arben, you are new. After you have had some experience we'll talk about it.' (Gingold had told me to address him as Dr. instead of Maestro) so I said: 'Dr. Szell, there are two kinds of violinists: those who learn, learn quickly; the others never learn.' I got the raise. When I received my first check (Trogdon, the personnel manager handed it to us once a week) I opened the envelope and saw there was so little money after taxes that I went back to Trogdon and said: 'Keep the check. I am very happy here. I don't need the money.' So Trogdon who was 6'5" — a big guy, looked at me as though I were wild. He wouldn't take it. It took two weeks of negotiating with me to cash the check. I said: 'I'm not complaining. I'm very happy here. It's not much money. I don't need it.' I lied. I needed it."

At this point I reminded David of the miserable apartment he lived in during his first season in Cleveland. "Yes, that was so. I moved around a lot. I used to go to the Salvation Army and buy a bed, a table and a chair. When I left in April or May, I left the apartment and all the furniture. I left everything. Nobody could find me. They were great days. I had a fabulous time there."

I asked David whether he appreciates those times more now seeing them from a different perspective. He told me he was lucky with Szell and then tried to recall his stand partner when he sat on sixth stand. I interrupted and suggested it was Sam Salkin but he quickly said: "No, Sam I know. He burned his pants waiting for the concert to begin in Oberlin. I told him there was smoke coming out of his pants. He put his hand in his pocket and took out his pipe and said to me: "It's my pipe" and he put it back in his pocket, a burning pipe! Meanwhile the concertmaster came out on stage, then Szell, and Salkin was on fire. He got up, ran off stage bumping into Szell on the way. It was a comedy. Sam was one of the nicest guys. He always wanted to have breakfast or lunch when we were on tour and I couldn't do it too well because when he would eat, his eggs would be on my shirt, on my face. He would spit when he talked. You couldn't tell him: you spit; don't spit, so I avoided him. I loved the guy. He used to fix watches. He had a little shop somewhere. He smoked cigarettes and when the ashes were about two inches long, he would open my watch. All the ashes would fall inside ruining the whole thing. Then he would say: 'your watch needs cleaning.'"

David remembered so vividly an experience on tour that was life altering for him. The orchestra was in Basel and played a Mozart piano concerto with Rudolph Serkin as soloist. After intermission the orchestra played the "Pastorale" symphony of Beethoven. "I started shaking and thought I was coming down with a cold or flu but I had never heard such music in my life. Something special was happening. After the concert the entire orchestra was shaking. Everyone. Szell said something to us: 'For forty years I have had a vision of how the Pastorale should be played, should sound. It only materialized tonight.' Now I hear the Pastorale and it's not the same. I was poisoned with this thing. I don't know what...but I was shaking."

How well I remember that only he could conduct the "Pastorale" and, for that matter, only he could conduct the "Death and Transfiguration" of Strauss. David recalled when he was in the Philadelphia Orchestra and Anshel Brushilow, its new concertmaster, was interviewed on live television, he was asked to indicate the greatest performance he had ever experienced. "Unhesitatingly he said: 'Without doubt, George Szell in Basel, with the Pastorale Symphony!'" David called Anshel after that interview and said: "My god, you are killing yourself before you start. If Ormandy hears the interview he won't like it. He hates Szell."

We agreed that no one could equal certain of Szell's interpretations. David summed up: "Certain things he did, no one could match. That is why the Cleveland Orchestra was considered the best American orchestra... and it was."

Rodney Van Sickle, Bass, 1957-1959

Rodney recalls being on tour in New York and standing in front of the Wellington Hotel with a few other orchestra members. Suddenly Szell came charging out of the hotel. There was a police car standing at the curb. Szell jumped in the back seat and said: "46th and Seventh, please." The cop just looked at him incredulously and said: "What? Who are you, mister? Get out of here."

Several months later because of personnel complications, Szell had to let Van Sickle go. He was apologetic and told Rodney he didn't deserve it from a playing point of view and offered to call William Steinberg in Pittsburgh. He "commanded me to audition there. I did and was hired. Szell was the supreme god.

"Since I've retired I have a lot more time to listen to music. If I can find a Szell/Cleveland recording I get it because those are some of the finest ever. I really appreciate it now."

Marc Lifschey, Oboe, 1950-1959; 1960-1965
Letter from his wife, Paula Lifschey

Dear Larry:

Marc died on Election Day 2000, so your letter arrived close to the eve of the fourth anniversary of that sad event. My last words to him were a lie: "Gore won." When he didn't respond, I knew it was all over. Since I didn't know Marc in his Szell days, all I have are his versions of the Szell stories. I know that he had great respect for Szell as a musician on one hand, but at times he felt he had to hold his playing in a vise. He talked about one conversation they had wherein Szell said: "Just don't be meshuga" and Marc said: "Just leave me alone and let me play." And another wherein Szell said to him: "I have destroyed people for less than the way you talked to me today."

Let's see — other tidbits — Szell telling him he shouldn't wear brown shoes; telling him how to breathe in the mountain air while on an orchestra tour crossing the Alps, stories about other musicians and Szell such as Anshel Brushilow saying: "If you ever speak to me like that again, I'll smash a chair over your head" or something to that effect; the Heifetz story, when there was a snow avalanche on the roof over the stage, but no one knew what the sound was — Gingold dashed over to Heifetz and wrapped his arms around him protectively. Szell fled the stage. "The captain deserted the ship," Marc would say with glee. He loved telling the story of how, in anticipation of Heifetz's first appearance with the Cleveland Orchestra, Szell asserted, "He won't frighten **me!**"

The line Rosenberg left out of his "Cleveland Orchestra Story" about Marc's departure from Cleveland was Marc standing up and saying: "Fourteen years of this shit" and then walking off stage. Myron Bloom said, when he spoke at Marc's memorial, that later he heard Szell say to someone: "This is the end of great orchestral playing in America."

As for the heart of what you are asking, though Marc had nothing positive to say about the relationship, the very fact of the tumultuous, emotionally charged way he spoke about him revealed, in my view, a far less simple picture, one partly colored by Marc's extreme resistance to a domineering personality that reminded him of his mother.

As you probably know, Marc's reputation meant more to everyone else than to him. He just wanted to enjoy the job, and though his official letter to the management when he left for the Metropolitan Opera job stated his father's illness as the reason, he simply wanted to get away from Szell. In fact, his father was horrified that he left Cleveland. But Marc loved opera. He said that being around singers reminded him of what he felt was important in his playing. When he allowed Szell to lure him back to Cleveland, he told his then-wife Cathy: "I just made the worst mistake of my life."

Thanks for getting in touch. It helps me to know that people still think of Marc.

All the best, Paula

Myron Bloom, Horn, 1954-1977

In chatting with Mike one day he told me what it meant to work with Szell and why Szell was so important to him personally. First he told me a story about his young life when his parents insisted that he attend a concert given by the famed cellist Emanuel Feuermann. "I had no interest in music but they prevailed upon me to go. When I came out of that concert I knew what I wanted to do with my life." Later he discovered that Szell was the pianist who played for Feuermann on some of his European tours.

Mike soon acquired all the Feuermann recordings. "He was my hero and has remained so my whole life. I wanted to be a cellist but became a horn player and always felt I played the cello on the horn. I played the horn with the ideas of string playing in my mind rather than the ideas of wind playing."

Myron was one of the few players raised in Cleveland so playing in the orchestra was a homecoming especially because he felt that Szell carried on the same tradition that had nurtured him in his formative years. Despite his initial fear when he first got into the orchestra, he admitted that he was pretty cocky. The orchestra was on tour in Worcester, Massachusetts and Mike was playing third horn. Szell asked to see him before the concert. "I walked into his room holding a cigarette. He looked at me and I looked at him. He didn't say a word and I didn't say a word. I couldn't understand what he wanted. I quickly went for an ashtray and snuffed it out. Then he said: 'You must have been quite a star in your former orchestra but I want you to know that in this orchestra I am the star.' My stomach was in an uproar."

I thought Szell understood the horn quite well but Mike explained that it was the music he understood well. "When we were in Vienna a man approached me and said: 'I taught Szell the horn and he sounded like a motorcycle.' He couldn't play the horn at all." "But," I persisted, "he certainly must have known the fingering." Mike said that was nonsense. "He knew about the music and everything about the orchestra. He had a concept of the orchestra that I really don't think anybody else ever had. **Ever.**"

I encouraged Mike to expand on this idea. He said Szell believed that tonal quality, intonation, dynamics, articulation and rubato must be engrained to begin making music. One of the things that bothered Szell about most American orchestras was the chasm existing between the winds and strings. Szell tried to close the gap by having gifted wind players who were as Gingold used to say: "the jewels in our orchestra."

I was reminded of my own experience when I first joined the orchestra. Technically I had to concern myself with a kind of articulation I had never experienced or thought of before. It was very, very crisp and seemed far more like wind articulation than the legato most string players used. When I expressed that to Mike he was reminded of Szell and Alexander Schneider who were at each others' throats quite a bit. Szell said to him: "You don't have any staccato." Schneider replied: "You don't have any legato."

Mike talked about Szell's favorite soloists: Casadesus, Fournier, and Serkin. When Casadesus came, Szell would rehearse the orchestra exactly in the style of

Casadesus. When Serkin came, he would rehearse in the style of Serkin, exactly. We exchanged thoughts about some of Szell's recordings. Mike was particularly impressed with Szell's recordings with Szigeti, two LPs of Mozart. I thought about the wonderful times with Serkin when we went to the very heart, the core of the music. Speaking of Serkin brought forth thoughts of Marlboro. "I was not so thrilled with Marlboro," said Mike. "There were Cleveland Orchestra players there who spoke about Szell with very little respect. I was infuriated." At that point I couldn't help but tell Mike that many people had trouble with Szell's personality.

Mike acknowledged that was true. "But it's like not seeing the forest for the trees. There it was, right in front of our eyes. I feel his presence every day of my life."

Richard Mackey, Horn, 1955-1963

After so many interviews with people who told me what a kindly old gentleman he was, I couldn't help but remark to Richard that Szell was more than formidable. Hell, he used to peel our skin off right in front of everybody. It didn't bother him at all to crucify someone in public. Many of the interviewees said they "heard" he could be a bastard but "he was always nice to me." So I asked Richard what experience he had.

He freely admitted that he couldn't say Szell was always nice to him. "When he liked you, he called you by your first name. Otherwise you were just 'third horn.' Clarity was the key word. He asked the horns to play louder than most orchestras at times. He liked to get that edge on the sound, that buzz. In a way, that was exciting but I don't think any other conductor asked us to play so loud."

He also recalled that the orchestra was required to wear shirt and tie to rehearsals and always on tour. This is unheard of today. No one would presume to tell orchestra members how to dress for rehearsal. "He sent Charlie Brennand to his hotel room to change his shirt after he caught him on the elevator wearing a tee shirt."

Richard loved the 1957 tour. He eagerly began to name all the cities in order: "Antwerp, Brussels, Bremem ...flying over on KLM. The Old Man met us at the airport in Brussels. Audiences were so enthusiastic. In Posnan, they applauded for a half hour and when we left the hall they were still applauding out by the stage door. I remember I cracked a note in the Brahms Symphony. When he saw me the next day at the airport, Szell said: 'That was a perfect missed note.'"

Richard recalled what a wonderful pianist Szell was and how he loved to tell soloists what to do. "He could be very rough on them. Jimmy Levine didn't like the way Szell treated the orchestra. As music director of the Boston Symphony (Richard now plays there) Levine doesn't treat an orchestra like that. The act of conducting did not come easily to Szell. Many conductors are more graceful and easier to follow, but so what. Szell got his musicians to play the way they did often through force of will but what he asked for was musically logical and he had talented musicians who wanted to play that way. He wasn't fighting the orchestra. They agreed with his ideas."

Sidney Weiss, Violin, 1956-1966

Sid told me his version of the Andre Previn story that has circulated for years in various forms. Sid was in a cab with Previn and "this is how I remember it. We were talking about Szell when I happened to mention the story about someone playing for him on his coffee table. Previn said: 'Wait a minute. That's me.' I said: 'Really? Well, now I can get the true story at last.'" So this is my recollection of what he told me:

Previn was a teenager making a career as a pianist and film composer. His agent got him a big break to play with Szell and the orchestra. Szell required every soloist to come a week before the first rehearsal so he could work over the piece with him. Previn arrived at the appointed time at Szell's home. Szell ushered him into the living room where they sat down on the couch. Szell took out his score and said: 'Well, let's begin.'

The piece was one that started with the piano and not the orchestra. So Previn asked: "Mr. Szell, where is your piano?" He replied: "You don't need a piano. Use the coffee table." Previn thought he couldn't be serious but poised his hands above the table and came down on the first chord. Szell said: "No, no, stop! It's too loud." Previn couldn't believe this and said to him: "You have to understand, Mr. Szell, that I'm not used to your coffee table." Szell gave him a dirty look and said: "I have no patience for smart alecks. Get out." He threw him out! Previn said: "I didn't know what to do. I went back to my hotel room totally stunned. Soon my agent called from New York." Apparently Szell had already called the agent who told Previn to come home. He was finished.

One of my favorite stories about Szell and Sid Weiss was when Sid auditioned with an instrument he had made himself. I asked Sid to share that with me: "I was auditioning for advancement in the section. I had purchased a Strad not long before and recently made a copy of it. I was really happier with the copy than I was with the Strad so when the time came to audition, I used my own instrument. Off stage before the audition, Druian asked me which instrument I was using. I said: 'This is one of my own instruments.' He was very distressed and thought that I should use the Strad. He had already told Szell I had purchased a Strad and was going to use it. 'Don't say anything," I suggested. 'He won't know the difference.' So I played and Szell was satisfied.

I was eager to tell the story the way I remembered it: You knew that Druian was angry. Mr. Szell stopped you and asked: "Mr. Weiss, what is this instrument you're playing?" You said: "It's a Weiss, Mr. Szell." Szell went through his formidable memory of all the books of violin makers, got to the "Ws" and couldn't find anyone listed by the name of Weiss so he said: "Veiss, Veiss, WHO is this Veiss?" And in your tiniest voice you said: "It's me, Mr. Szell, I made it myself." Szell then countered: "**But that's impossible!**" In Szell's eyes you were a violinist, not a violin maker. How could you do both?

"I guess that's the way it was," conceded Sid. "It jogs my memory." Then I remembered that Sid Weiss was also connected with the famous Jack Benny concert held at Severance Hall to benefit the Pension Fund. Benny, ever the great comedian, came out on stage and teased Szell quite a bit. Szell tried gamely but really didn't know how to take it. He was prepared to conduct seriously for this famous amateur violinist who immediately captivated the audience with his humor. Finally Benny seemed ready to play but he made many false starts laced with pranks, puzzling and frustrating Szell. Szell would raise his arms to give a downbeat, then Benny would stop and delight the audience with another joke. Finally, Benny raised his arms to perform, but he had forgotten his bow. Nonetheless, from off stage came this marvelous virtuoso playing.

At this point in the story, Sid interrupted and said: "I think you've got it a little wrong. I'll tell you what happened. Benny stopped and said: 'I need a music stand. Can someone bring me a music stand?' And he looked toward backstage. Szell had me play this part. I was backstage and dressed like a stagehand. My shirt was hanging out of my pants. I brought out a music stand and as Benny was adjusting the stand, he said: 'Hold my fiddle and don't put your hands on the bow hair.' I took his fiddle and bow while he fussed with the music stand. Then I put the fiddle under my chin and played a virtuoso passage soaring all over the fiddle. He stopped and gave me his famous look, took the fiddle out of my hands and said: 'Get out.' Benny owned a beautiful Strad, which he left to the Los Angeles Philharmonic when he died. Their concertmaster now plays it."

I asked Sid what he thought accounted for Szell's success with the orchestra. "One word: **Fear**. Let's face it. There was no union support, no right of appeal." But, of course, there was more. Sid agreed that Szell strove for clarity and transparency in his music making and spoke of all the rehearsal time Szell demanded. This would not happen today. Concerts were usually sold out and the management desperately wanted to add a concert to the series each week but Szell would not hear of it because it would mean giving up one of his rehearsals. It was six rehearsals and three concerts.

Sid spoke to me of the human side of George Szell, which was less well known. There was an older Hungarian violinist in the orchestra named Jeno Antal who had once been a member of a famous quartet. He knew Szell in Hungary a long time ago and Sid thought he might have been instrumental in helping Szell when he was young. When Szell came to Cleveland he gave "Yanshe" a job with the orchestra. "When I came," Sid goes on, "he had been in the orchestra a number of years already. Yanshe had a congenital eye disorder, which was hereditary and incurable. Little by little, he was going blind and couldn't see the music the way he should — he told me this himself — so he went to Szell and told him there was no point in his continuing. This is the amazing thing: Szell said to him: 'I know your wife is ill, you have problems and you need this job very badly. You need a paycheck. I'm putting you in the back of the second violins where you will be inconspicuous. Put soap on your bow and just listen carefully. Be careful you don't look like you are playing when no one else is. Just fake it.' But Yanshe was a very conscientious gentle man. He said: 'That's very kind but I would be too ashamed.' So he didn't do it and left the orchestra. I don't know how he managed financially after that. Perhaps Szell arranged some settlement because there were no pensions then."

Stanley Maret, Contrabassoon, 1962-1997

Stanley spent eight years under Szell's direction. George Goslee was on stage with him during his audition and, "so to speak, turned pages. He was telling me what to play. I don't recall Szell saying a word to me. But I definitely felt his presence."

Stanley described being overwhelmed by the power and beauty, the precision of the orchestra. "The musicians were all around me and I was very impressed with all of them." He described his fear and that of those around him when Szell was angry but he could only remember one incident when Szell actually blew up. It was when the orchestra was threatening to strike. Szell, he described, "said in a very loud voice: '**Remember, I am your friend.**'"

In Stanley's opinion it was the tip of Szell's stick that made all the difference. All one had to do was follow his stick. "I would not play too fast or too slowly. It was precision. That stick was like a god to me."

Bob Pangborn, Percussion, 1957-1963

The Cleveland Orchestra was Bob's first major job. His audition with Szell, Cloyd Duff and Olin Trogden went very well and he was offered a contract. He was overwhelmed when Szell first came on stage: "I used to see him from a little hole in the acoustical shell behind the percussion section. I would stand there and look through that hole when I was a student." He was very nervous at his first rehearsal but the beautiful sound of the orchestra gave him the determination to do an outstanding job. "Hearing players like Marc who is still the finest oboe sound ever — he set the standard — I was very excited."

In his second season, Szell decided to program the "Lieberman Concerto for Basel Drum and Orchestra" which is a loud, bombastic piece and Bob was given the solo part. After the first performance, Szell called him downstage to take a bow, which surprised him. "I remember bowing and turning around to leave the stage. He motioned me to go ahead. As I passed him, my intention was to pat him on the back as a thank-you gesture. He was so tall that I ended up patting him on the ass! When I realized what happened, I started to shake. I was petrified but nothing came of it. That was my only solo performance!

"I had great respect for Szell's intellect. He wanted the orchestra to play everything very precisely as if it were a large string quartet. Good balance was important to him. I could never decide if he achieved his goals due to fear or respect or a combination of both. Hanging around with Marc, I got used to 'Cyclops' staring him down in a solo. In 'Don Juan' Szell would try to conduct every nuance. Marc would just put his head down and not look at him, which infuriated Szell. It was a love/hate relationship.

"When I left the orchestra he had been putting me under a great deal of pressure because of the Bartok Concerto for Orchestra."

What a horror that turned out to be for the percussionists. Bob Matson played it beautifully but Szell took him off the part and assigned it to Pangborn. "Szell screwed around with different sticks and mallets, the sound and the drums, and it was crazy. He knew what he wanted to hear but he really couldn't convey his idea to us. What was so mysterious? It was a snare drum without snares, an open sounding drum with a drumstick and he was trying to make something else out of it. It was a nightmarish experience."

I could verify that. It was hell for all of us and we weren't in Bob's shoes. Pangborn had nightmares over it for years. He hadn't planned to leave the orchestra. It was after that event that the orchestra played at Smith College. Bob admits that he was not totally happy with his performance there but when Szell called him in they had a scene. After that it was nothing but agony. One piece we did had a glockenspiel part that was touchy. "In rehearsal Szell stopped and wanted to hear the glockenspiel part again. I played it perfectly. So he wanted to hear it again, play it this way, and then again. I am sure the whole intention was to work me down until I would make a mistake. Son of a gun. I set my jaw, ground my teeth and didn't make any mistakes. He finally moved on and didn't prove what he was trying to prove. Later I got a notice that I wasn't going to be rehired. As for the Bartok fiasco: Cloyd ended up playing it on a regular snare drum with a snare drum stick. None of this bullshit. He just played it."

Meanwhile the orchestra committee went to Szell and persuaded him to reverse his decision and rehire Bob. But Bob remembered what happened to Harry Herforth who had had a similar situation over the coronet solo in "La Mer." Szell rehired him for another year and then he was gone. So Bob went on to the Met and later became principal percussionist of the Detroit Symphony where he remains to this day.

He recalled one more incident when he was home on leave from the service. He was back to that hole in the stage set at Severance and the orchestra was doing a piece with a big chime part. As Bob Matson was playing the chimes, the hammer end of the chime mallet came off, flew up in the air and landed right next to the podium. "It's a shame it didn't hit him" he told me with a smile in his voice.

Before my interview with Pangborn, I had spoken with Bob Matson who suffered terribly in the orchestra. Someone said when they called him, he answered the phone saying: "This is the former Bob Matson."

Robert Matson, Percussion, 1952-1989

"Anything I could say to you about George Szell, you couldn't possibly print in your book."

Alfred Genovese, Oboe, 1959-1960

After a concert when the orchestra was in Elmira, New York, a few of the players joined Al at an Italian joint. Al had linguini with clam sauce. During the night he became very ill so in the morning he went to the hotel dining room to get some coke or ginger ale. "I walked into the dining which had just opened and Ben Selzcer, the violist, was there. He said: 'My god, Al, what happened? You look like you have just been run over.' Soon Szell walked in, noticed me in the same condition and panicked, probably thinking he would be without a principal oboe that night. He exclaimed: **'What happened?'** I explained it to him and he wanted to know who had been there with me and where I had eaten. I told him to which he responded: 'Ha! Don't you know they don't know how to make that stuff here. The way to make good clam sauce, first you get the olive oil and cut up some garlic...he proceeded to give me the recipe which just made me sicker. I said: 'Please stop talking.' He laughed and thought it was funny."

Al's audition with Szell seemed interminable to him. "I wasn't playing the whole time. We would sit, talk, I'd play again. John Mack had already auditioned and Szell had told him he thought he would have the job. Szell had one more person to hear and Mack asked who that might be. Szell said: 'Alfred Genovese.' Mack told me many years later that his stomach sank. That was a compliment, you know."

Even now Al says he really misses Szell despite the fact that he was with Cleveland for only one year as Marc Lifschey's replacement. Marc had gone on to play at the Met. When Marc returned to Cleveland, Al then replaced him at the Metropolitan Opera Orchestra. Al was thinking of returning to Cleveland if the opportunity arose. Later when he went to Rudolph Bing to ask for a raise, Bing asked him: "Why would you want to go back to Cleveland? You'd be playing with George Szell again and you know how I feel about him." During a conversation with Bing someone said: "Szell is his own worst enemy." "Not while I'm alive," Bing replied.

Michael Grebanier, Cello, 1959-1963

In 1959 Michael was nineteen years old playing with the Pittsburgh Symphony. His teacher, Leonard Rose, advised him to audition for the Cleveland Orchestra. "I did the usual stuff and Szell offered me the job. That was the beginning of a bad relationship."

Szell insisted there was no need for a written contract but when Michael arrived in Cleveland he was sitting eighth chair instead of third chair as he had been promised. "I was not shy about expressing my displeasure and Szell didn't like it a bit. He said: 'You have to wait and leave it up to me.'"

Michael and I chatted about Szell's conducting technique. He felt Szell had a poor baton technique and that everything was over rehearsed, not leaving much for the moment. He often repeated the same repertoire and would begin rehearsing a new piece weeks in advance. The only exceptions to his didactic approach were Dvorak and Schumann, in Michael's opinion.

Michael talked about the time Szell became incensed by the uncontrolled coughing in the audience. He raised his arms to give the downbeat, lowered them again to wait for the coughing to subside, did it again to no avail and finally turned to the audience and said: "I'll give you just five minutes to stop your coughing." and left the stage in a rage. When he returned he was greeted with embarrassed laughter and some booing.

Michael remembered the tale that Alice referred to in her interview. "Szell's first wife had remarried. She and her husband, cellist, Bernard Heifetz, came to a Cleveland Orchestra concert in Long Island and sat in the front row behind the podium. Szell strode to the podium, turned to face the audience and noticed his ex-wife. The look on his face was priceless. When he turned to the orchestra he looked stunned.

"My personal relationship with him really soured when he wanted me to sign a long term contract. He said he had plans for me to become principal. He goaded Frezin into resigning and me into signing a long-term contract. But when the next season began he had hired Jules Eskin as principal. I was really pissed and let him know it, which didn't make him happy. He said that I was cutting my own throat. He took me out of recordings with Casadesus and I knew I had to get out of there. I was offered a job in St. Louis as principal but it was after the deadline when one could tender a resignation. I asked Szell to relieve me of my contract. He said: 'NO, a contract is a contract.' He refused to let me go. It was not a good relationship."

Arnold Steinhardt, Violin, 1959-1964

Szell was one of the judges of the Leventritt competition, which Arnold won. Basically that competition became Arnold's audition. Not only did Szell arrange for Arnold to study with Szigeti in Switzerland but he paid for the trip as well. While he was there, Szell checked up on him and came to visit once in his black Cadillac. It was identical to the huge black Cadillac he drove at home and was completely out of place in Switzerland. "Szigeti lived up in the foothills with narrow, winding roads overlooking Lake Geneva. Szell was not a good driver. He invited me to go out. I was incredibly honored that he would spend time with me but it was the ride of terror. Other cars had to drive off the road to make way for him but he was oblivious — a bit like Mr. Magoo."

Arnold recalls his first rehearsal. "Even in my excitement I noticed the heaviness in Severance Hall as we awaited Szell's arrival — the kind of atmosphere one feels before a summer storm. At 10 a.m. sharp the maestro mounted the podium with a 'Good morning, ladies and gentlemen, Brahm's First.' There had been no stragglers and little talk beforehand...but finally, it was intermission. At twenty-two, I was the youngest player in the orchestra. How nice, I thought, a welcoming committee. In truth, however, Sam Salkin, first violin, tried to sell me a watch; Ed Matey, second violin, offered me mutual funds; Irv Nathanson, double bass, wondered if I needed instrument insurance; and Angie Angelucci, French horn, tried to sell me a Plymouth. The Cleveland Orchestra's slim thirty-two week season allowed me, as a bachelor, the luxury of spending my summers in Marlboro, but most of the orchestra, with families to feed, did what they could to make a living. I didn't buy the watch; I did buy mutual funds and insurance. I did not buy the Plymouth. Two out of four wasn't bad."

Szell gave Arnold much encouragement and a certain amount of grief. "I was very young even for my age. I had to show up on time with the right music learned — normal expectations — but I was an undisciplined kid who found himself in a spit-polished, crack unit, if not the world's greatest orchestra, which I would argue it was. Szell would wonder why I was there at the last moment, not fifteen minutes earlier to warm up.

"We had many conversations about music, I played concertos and studied music with him. It showed me a side of him that I rarely saw when he was on the podium. Yes, he could be expansive and tell a joke once in a while, but normally I wouldn't call him relaxed. At these private sessions he would sit at the piano playing the orchestral reduction and relax. He would say: 'Why are you so stiff in that cadenza? You should be having fun.' Then he'd play a free flowing, elegant, light cadenza for me at the piano. I was always shocked because this seemed so out of character. He chose not to show that essential side of his nature often. The orchestra would go on tour and play a great symphony. He'd tighten all the bolts so that it was beautifully executed, but occasionally didn't have the freedom some of us would have liked. Every once in a while, though, he'd just let go. When that happened... my gosh. Then it was like the Eroica — never to forget! I especially loved doing the Tchaikovsky symphonies with him."

Szell used to get on Arnold's case because his socks would fall down and show the white skin of his legs as he stretched them out toward the podium. One day Szell brought Arnold into his office and showed him the garter belt system that held up his socks. "Then he gave me a long lecture about how I should do this. I never took his advice but from that moment on I made sure my socks were up!" Szell called Arnold into his office many times, some times to tell him about music he should study or books he should read or to complain about the way he had played pizzicato.

During my interviews I found so many people remembering the same stories, each told in a slightly different way but so indelibly printed on the orchestra psyche. One was the time on tour when the orchestra was alternating two different programs. One began with the prelude to "Lohengrin" by Wagner, the other with the overture to the "School for Scandal" by Barber. As Arnold told it: "The Lohengrin begins with four first violins playing harmonics very high and very quietly. For this Szell had to give a beautiful, ethereal sort of indication, but the School for Scandal required a furious downbeat. We were playing in Allentown, Pennsylvania and it was time for the Lohengrin. Szell walked out on stage and bowed. We all placed our hands (first violins) way up high to make sure to find the notes and were all poised with the bow. He turned to the orchestra and gave this violent downbeat for the other program and all our bows bounced as if it were an 8.5 on the Richter scale as they skidded across the strings. He realized immediately what had happened and switched gears. When the piece was finished he bowed, and walking past us said: 'They must think I'm mad.' Off stage he said to someone: 'Well, at least they're both in the same key.'"

At recording sessions, Szell and Howard Scott, the Columbia Records producer, had a system of communication. Szell had a phone on the podium which kept buzzing. He'd pick it up and they would talk. Arnold tells of the time Szell picked it up at the end of a long session: "We were all sort of numb by then. From the center of the orchestra Marc said: 'Hello, Mother.' The whole orchestra collapsed — even Szell laughed."

I recalled a major incident with Henryk Szeryng. A month before he came to play with the orchestra in Carnegie Hall he came to Cleveland to perform. It was obvious Szell and Szeryng did not get along from the start. Arnold suggested that there was something very off-putting about Szeryng's manner that he was slightly balmy but it just translated when you first met him as arrogance. In the Severance Hall rehearsals, Szell stopped him and said: "We don't play like that in Cleveland. Your playing is beneath our standard." Szeryng handled it very well. He nodded and we continued. Szell stopped again, railed at him and accused him of all manner of things. About the third time Szell shouted: **"This is the Cleveland Orchestra!** If this tastelessness doesn't change I'm canceling the concerto," and he stormed off stage. Szeryng kept his cool. Somehow the newspapers got a hold of the incident and reporters rushed to Severance Hall to talk to Szell who slammed his door in their faces so they found Szeryng and said to him: "We understand you are a wonderful violinist and have been treated cruelly by Mr. Szell." Szeryng answered calmly: "Where did you hear such a thing? Mr. Szell has always been kind to me. I think of him as a father and masterful teacher." Then, of course, when we did the concert, Szell steamed every moment.

The Carnegie Hall concert came about a month and a half later. Szeryng came on stage and Szell was ready for him. Maybe it was the best conducting he ever did, technically. He somehow managed to get the orchestra, as he would say, at 'sixes and sevens' with the soloist, so no matter what Szeryng did, he always sounded slightly wrong and the orchestra sounded exactly right. Szeryng got terrible reviews. It was his New York debut.

"If you analyze this," Arnold said: "Szeryng dealt with this incident perfectly. It was ingenious, an absolutely incredible act of diplomacy. He could have lashed out and no one would have blamed him. He was a weird guy. I got to know him a little better later on. He came to play a recital the first year I was in Cleveland. It was fabulous. Joe Gingold and I went to the concert together. Szeryng was standing at the back corner of the stage after the concert. Joe and I mounted the front of the stage to approach him. There were a few people surrounding Szeryng. He raised his arm in a theatrical salute and said across the stage loudly in his Polish accent: 'Josef Kinkol, my best friend in America.' Joe whispered softly so only I could hear: 'He's a wonderful violinist but do I have to be his best friend in America?'"

This was the time of cultural exchange with the Soviet Union. Szell was anxious for the orchestra to participate in this unique opportunity. He seemed a bit nervous around violinist David Oistrach *(pictured)* who was an important artist on the world scene and the number one cultural export of the Soviet Union. During this time Rostropovich first performed with us. He spoke no English so Albert Michelson had to translate for him. As Arnold recalled: "After the rehearsal he expressed interest in trying the cellos in our section. He wanted to know the quality of the cellos in an American orchestra. He played each cello one by one and every one sounded like it had an amplifier."

Arnold also recalled Milstein being bored at least once in rehearsal because Szell constantly stopped to pick on the orchestra. "At one point Szell again found fault with the woodwinds and stopped the orchestra and the soloist. However, some of the players didn't stop immediately. He held up his hand to the first violin section to motion them to be quiet. As he began to speak to the woodwind section his palm went right in front of Milstein's face. Milstein looked at the palm, then turned to look at us with a smirk on his face. He then took his bow and stuck the tip of it into Szell's palm. Szell stopped in mid-sentence looking startled as if to say: what is this guy, a madman?!"

People often asked Arnold what he learned from being in the orchestra and working for Szell. He would reply that he learned how to tie a bow tie and how to play poker. Szell was happy about the bow tie but not so about the poker. "His design for me was that of an artist/musician who cultivated only good habits and playing poker was not one of them. According to him, I was associating with the wrong people in the orchestra."

Arnold told me a personal story of Szell's phenomenal memory: "In my first private conversation with him, he asked many questions about my background and my parents. I wondered what that was all about. He asked my father's first name which was Mischa and what he did. I told him my dad had a small liquor store in downtown Los Angeles and he wanted to know where it was. I told him. That year passed, another year passed. I think it was in my third year with the orchestra that Szell called me in and said: 'Arnold, I couldn't find your dad's store.' I said: '**What?**' He said: 'I looked for a liquor store on Eighth and Figaro and found one that said **Mitchell's Liquor Store** but not **Mischa's**'. It turned out that my dad decided to call it **Mitchell's** because he felt **Mischa's** was too exotic a name for downtown LA. Szell had a mind like a steel trap."

It's been many years since Szell's death and I can't believe how often he enters my mind and even my dreams. Arnold acknowledged that this was true for him as well: "Still once or twice a year I dream about him. Isn't that amazing? A guy with that kind of personality made his way into the interior of our existence. It's too bad you couldn't interview his wife, Helene." That was so true because she was an interesting person. To me she was a sort of Marlene Dietrich type. She and Szell seemed good together. When he would get out of control she was the only one who could deal with him.

I asked Arnold if he recalled a certain well-known seafood restaurant in Hartford. Indeed he did: "When our train doors opened we would tear over there like fiends, Szell included. This story I heard happened before I came into the orchestra: Szell asked the waiter: 'What is the fresh fish?' The young waiter told him what there was and Szell said: 'Is it really fresh?' 'Yes, sir, it is,' replied the waiter. Szell insisted: 'I want you to look me in the eye and tell me that. Is it fresh?' The waiter looked Szell in the eye, getting more and more uncomfortable and said: 'Yes, sir, it is fresh.' Then Szell reached in his wallet, took out a five dollar bill and handed it to him saying: 'Now, young man, is it or is it not fresh?' The kid said: 'I'm sorry, sir, it is not fresh.'"

I asked Arnold to tell me about the times he performed as soloist with the orchestra. "The crowning achievement for me was playing the Beethoven Concerto with Szell and the orchestra. We had piano rehearsals beforehand. Rehearsing the Mozart concertos in his studio were unforgettable sessions. It was a different Szell in terms of music making. When he sat down at the piano demonstrating, he was very impressive, very inspiring. But when it came to Beethoven, he clamped down. I wanted to play freely and he wouldn't allow it. We had fights over that, not big fights, but I resisted and he pushed. In retrospect, I think of that time in relation to my own students who sometimes play all over the place. For instance, there is a G minor section in the first movement that is extremely touching. If you play it beautifully and classically, it can be moving. If you get carried away and begin to sentimentalize the thing, it weakens it. That's what I wanted to do, to play it much slower and infuse in it all kinds of feeling. Now when I hear my students doing that, I feel like I am Szell. I tell them: You can't do that."

We then discussed the level of playing in orchestras today. To me, it seems, we now have very competent players but not as many unique personalities. Arnold agreed and thought that the level of playing had gone up. "You don't get the weak players that you occasionally got in the old days. On the other hand, I don't know if you would get anybody like Bob Marcellus and certainly not Marc."

"No, never Marc…never in any age."

I suggested that he might want to get the recording of Marc's performance of the Bach Cantata with Mack Harrell singing and Bob Shaw conducting.

"I have it," said Arnold. "In fact, it is in my car. I don't want to play it too often. It's too beautiful. In fact, it's a miracle, it is a fucking miracle. It undoes me."

With that we both choked up, unable to speak for what seemed like minutes.

Touring the Soviet Union – 1965

The fifties and sixties were perilous and tense times for the world in general and the two combative superpowers in particular. It was the heart of the Cold War. Countries of middle Europe were choked by the steel hand of their controllers in Moscow. There were uprisings, "revolutions," in Poland, Hungary and Czechoslovakia. The world stood at the brink of extinction by nuclear weapons in the hands of a suicidal aggressor. But there was a bright ray of hope and it was held in the hands of artists and musicians on both sides of the Iron Curtain.

The idea appealed to authorities in both East and West. It was thought that if artists of the very highest level were to be seen and heard by people of the opposing countries it would put a better face on things, softening, humanizing. And there were amazing artists to be exchanged. The project met with real success until an American spy plane was shot down over Russia. Summarily, it died and didn't begin again until the early sixties when Cleveland began to share its Severance Hall stage with astounding artists like Oistrach, Gilels and Rostropovich. Audiences were stunned, recordings and personal friendships were made. Szell was having the time of his life making incredible music and showing off his one of a kind orchestra to new Russian friends. These relationships led to a tour of unsurpassed political and artistic significance. At the invitation of Moscow's Kremlin and with the sponsorship of the United States State Department the orchestra undertook its longest, most adventurous and arguably most successful tour, winning thousands of new friends and giving a new look to the face of America.

Yuri - Who Is This Guy?

It was our first evening in Moscow. The trip had been exhausting. Our Pan Am 707 had stopped in London to pick up a Russian crew with the codes to get us safely past Soviet radar defenses. Several buses brought us to the Leningradskya Hotel. Each bus had a host from Intourist, the travel bureau, or Gosconcert, the concert organization. It was their job to welcome us and accompany us to the hotel. I heard soon that a few musicians on one of the buses were quite uncomfortable with their host. His English was crisp and his humor edgy.

In the lobby I was watching the hotel's only television set, a small black and white high above the desk. Clearly it was the evening news broadcast and though I could not understand the language, I could tell something major had happened as the newsman said: "North Vietnam...President Johnson" in an excited voice. Just then I noticed a young man, neatly dressed, chatting with a few of our musicians, completely at ease with English. So I went over to him and during a lull in the conversation I asked about the news broadcast. He drew himself to his full height, paused and began: "Today your B52 bombers have begun to bomb North Vietnam. They are bombing hospitals... schools...orphanages...old folks homes...peasant villages...The whole world is enraged."

It seemed as though he would never stop. I kept thinking: who is this guy?...why is he doing this to me?...what is happening to the goodwill tour?...has it crashed before the very first concert? Then his voice changed, reflective, softened, and after a breath he said:

"But if no one gets too excited and presses any of the wrong buttons, in twenty-five years we'll all be worried about those crazy Chinese Communists!" My head was reeling. Before I could recover my balance there he was, brilliantly forecasting the future. Moreover, in the world's capitol of Communism I would never have expected to hear the words: "crazy" and "Communists" in the same sentence. Who is this guy!!! I decided to keep my distance, keep my curiosity in check.

But the next evening there he was again in conversation with several musicians. His English had a light British accent. From his conversation I learned he was twenty-three. At nineteen he had been with a government mission to Egypt. His vocabulary was richly layered. He used and understood American idioms with precision. Before I could stop I heard myself say: "How is it that you speak such fantastic English?" Quickly he replied: "Oh, that's easy...I went to spy school! The Foreign Language Institute is just three blocks down the street. That's where all the spies go to learn English.

Again I was stunned. Perhaps he was **the one**, the spy to watch over us to see who was up to no good. But do real spies say they went to spy school? Actually we enjoyed talking to each other and soon a friendship developed. Some of my colleagues were amused at our joking and hearty banter while others were not sure what to think. During the second or third week of our stay a colleague visited me in my hotel room in Tiblisi, Georgia. With a worried and serious expression he said: "You know...your friend...Reznikoff...?" "Yes," I said. "Well, you know he's..." "He's what?" "You know"..."Know what?"..."He's the **one**"... I strung him out forcing him to say it: "He's the **spy**!!! "SO," I said, "what is he going to learn from me, **the double bass bowings** of the orchestra? He can have them if he wants. **They're not so good anyway.**"

The evening after hearing the world news from Yuri Reznikoff was our first concert of the Soviet tour. Cultural exchanges had come to a complete stop between our countries for some time. This visit was the first of a new series of "Good Will" tours sponsored by the United States State Department and hosted by the Kremlin. The Cleveland's and Mr. Szell's reputations had preceded us. Excitement in the capitol city was such that all tickets for the first two of five concerts in Moscow's Conservatory Hall were taken by those with power and position in government or the military. But the international news cast a definite shroud over the audience's ability to welcome us and respond to the music. We were prepared as never before. Our performances were razor sharp technically and musically, but after brilliant performances of each work on the program I could see audience members glance at their neighbor to each side, and then looking straight ahead, clap hands just one chilling time. Still Szell and the orchestra would not give up trying to please this most difficult audience. Music from "Porgy Y Bess" was announced as an encore and we could hear a kind of gasp of pleasure and anticipation rise from the packed house. When the performance finished there was a roar of approval beyond any we had known. American music by Americans played for Russians — in Moscow! A politically safe story. Music, American music, with its roots in jazz! Everything they had held back through the evening was released and expressed with free, profound emotion. The ice was broken. The orchestra had just launched the most important, thrilling and successful tour of its history.

Several players had joined the orchestra between the European and Soviet tours. My interviews with some of them follow.

Diane Mather, Cello, 1963-2001
Robert Perry, Cello, 1968-1994
John Rautenberg, Flute, 1961-2005
Muriel Carmen, Viola, 1951-1994

John: Once when one of our horn players played a solo with vibrato, Szell said: "Please don't play the French horn with vibrato because if I'm going to listen to that I'll go to Paris where the restaurants are much better."

Diane: Let's talk about Szell's technique. We string players all laughed about his pizzicato conducting because he would just do something vague and we had to guess his intention. But we would always be there together. We were doing the Barber Piano Concerto with John Browning when Szell did one of those "things." Szell glanced over at me. I must have had a mystified look on my face. He kind of smiled. In the next measure there was another pizzicato and he looked right at me, gave a very clear gesture, and grinned.

Larry: Do you remember Helene, his wife? She was at a women's social gathering I am told and...married to this tall, commanding, highly regarded, highly publicized man, everyone wanted to know what her life with him was like. Someone suggested it must be very exciting to which she replied: "You know, my dear, it's not that glamorous. Before the concert, he's too nervous, and after the concert...he's too tired."

John: My mother started going to concerts before Severance Hall was built. When Szell came as guest conductor he conducted and played a Mozart piano concerto. After the concert, my mother and Moe Sharp's wife Betty (my mother's sister) told him how wonderful the concert was. He said: "Why, of course." They said the orchestra was transformed in the one week he was guest conductor. It was a miracle.

Larry: The orchestra had had a stream of mediocre conductors. Then he came in and it was a revelation. When he was appointed Music Director in Cleveland, it is my guess that his ambition was to become the leader of the New York Philharmonic but by the sixties the Cleveland Orchestra was so handmade to his own ideals that he realized he had achieved his desires right in Cleveland.

Bob: The orchestra would get a bit sloppy when he was gone too long. Once when he came back after a long period, he stopped a rehearsal and said: "Strings, you must play in tune. If not, you will be just like any other orchestra."

John: In the late sixties, Lynn Harrell was the newly appointed principal cellist. We were on tour in Boston and were flying to New York the next day when Lynn broke his ankle. He had to be loaded on the plane because he had a big cast. Szell was furious that Lynn had missed the concert in Boston because he had to have x-rays. Szell was seated in the same row across the aisle from Lynn. Harvey McQuire and I were sitting a row behind them. At first, Szell was silent but when we got up in the air he said to Lynn: "What happened?" Lynn replied: "I broke my ankle." "How did it happen?" inquired Szell to which Lynn responded: "I slipped on the ice." Szell said: "I'm sorry about that. Where did it happen?" Lynn: "On a street in Boston." Szell: "Yes, but what street?" Lynn: "I don't know the name of the street. I was just going for a walk." Szell: "What if you got lost? How could you get back to the hotel without the name of the street?" Lynn: "I would call a taxi. I knew the name of the hotel." So that calmed Szell for a while. He was fishing for an opening for his sword. A few minutes later he said: "Well, did this happen on the sidewalk or the street?" Lynn: "I was just stepping off the sidewalk into the street. Then I slipped on the ice and fell." Szell: "Oh, then, all right."

After a few minutes Szell said: "Were you wearing galoshes?" Lynn: "No, I was wearing my shoes." Szell spoke loudly: **"You shouldn't go out on an icy day without galoshes!"** Finally he had his chance. He lectured Lynn for ten minutes about galoshes and poor Lynn could only sit there and endure the barrage.

Muriel: On a train in Europe I was very thirsty. The water looked murky and to my surprise, Szell offered me a glass of scotch.

Larry: Really?

Muriel: I drank it. It wasn't exactly thirst quenching. But many years later leaving on tour from JFK, I noticed Szell had a bottle of scotch in his hand. He said: "Muriel, if you can remember where we were when I gave you that scotch, you can have this bottle." I couldn't remember, but he did.

Diane: After the Kent State shootings some of us were wearing black armbands and decided to wear them with our black concert clothes but were very apprehensive stepping out of uniform. As it happened, Szell came on stage, bowed and asked everyone to "Please join me in standing in simple human recognition of the tragic events of the past weekend."

Larry: I heard of many stories of events that occurred before I joined the orchestra. For instance, the orchestra was returning by train from a triumphant series of concerts at Carnegie Hall. The third horn player was reading the arts section of the Sunday Times, which had a column of tidbits. He came to a snippet stating that a well-known freelance horn player in the New York City area would be going to Cleveland to play third horn with the Cleveland Orchestra next year. He said aloud: "That's my job!" and ran to find Szell in another railcar. Showing him the newspaper he asked: "Is this true?" "You don't believe everything you read in the papers, do you?" Szell replied. Of course, then he felt much better. Two weeks later he got his notice.

Another tale was about a double bass player who was new to the orchestra. There was an opening with the Chicago Symphony in his home town. He thought he would audition but to be fair he told Szell that he was thinking of this. He also told Szell he liked Cleveland and was thinking of buying a house here but would like some notion of his long-term prospects. Szell cut in: "Real estate is always a good investment." So he stayed, bought a house and was relieved of his position!!! I then asked John about his invitation to play first flute in St. Louis.

John: We were on tour in New York. The concertmaster of the St. Louis Symphony came on stage at break, introduced himself to me and asked if I would be interested in the principal flute opening next season. I replied: "Maybe. When's the audition?" "Tomorrow morning," he said. I played the audition and they offered me the job. Back in Cleveland I went in to talk to Barksdale to tell him about the offer. He said he had to think about it, which meant he had to call Szell who was in Europe then. When I came in the next day to see Barksdale, he said: "Mr. Szell would like you to remain here in Cleveland. He considers you to be the next principal flutist of this orchestra." I asked him to put that in writing but, of course, he refused but he did change my title to Associate Principal so I stayed on.

Larry: I then asked about Szell's attitude toward women in the orchestra.

Muriel: He was fine. I think Alice was first. Evelyn was hired by Leinsdorf, and then I. I don't think he had any prejudice toward women at all. I think he would have hired women much sooner if it weren't for the trustees.

Diane: Evelyn felt she had to be very careful to set an example. She also thought she shouldn't have children because of her job. But I didn't get any feeling about women from him. Leonard Rose suggested I audition because Szell had told him there were a couple of openings. Rose said: "Just be polite and courteous as you are."

Muriel: We got the announcement of Szell's death backstage at Blossom. Louis told us. All the women were in tears.

Diane: We were stunned. I don't think anyone believed he could die.

Theodore Johnson, Clarinet, 1959-1995

Ted was called into Szell's office one of the first weeks he was in the orchestra. "During the concert we were doing a violin or piano concerto. There was no clarinet in the second movement so to pass the time I was reading the program which I had sitting on my knee. Szell kept staring at me but I couldn't understand why until he called me into his office and told me that I shouldn't have the program on my knee because it was distracting to the audience."

When I asked Ted about his first rehearsal with Cleveland, he said: "I was cocky and surprised how easy it was. In my previous position there were all kinds of problems around me. Suddenly I was in a situation where everyone knew his instrument and listened carefully. It was just like putting on a glove. It was tremendous. Bob Marcellus and I were a real fit. We could anticipate each other's phrasing and know exactly what the other was going to do."

Ted believed Szell's hiring procedures played a great part in his success. At Ted's audition, Szell spoke with him for about fifteen minutes about the latest book he had read and the reason he played a certain make instrument. "But the most interesting thing was that he asked Bob Marcellus to come out on stage. First I played a Mozart concerto and a few orchestral excerpts. But then Bob brought out music for all the important duo clarinet literature and we played together. Szell listened from the audience. He had instructed Bob to do certain things to see if I was capable of catching them. For instance, Bob would play a little faster than the normal tempo or he would play flat here and sharp there to see if I could catch it. He wanted to know how I blended with Bob so there were many times he would play with an edgier tone or a darker tone to see if I could match them. Szell hired people who were team people. Some players were actually better in audition than those he selected but he wanted team players.

I commented that unfortunately that ideal has been lost long ago.

Ted agreed. "Szell would hire team players and perfectionist personalities. He would insert himself as a father figure and then would hold a carrot just far enough in front of our noses and say it is almost 'fit for human consumption.' You would keep trying but could never really reach that carrot, but you would break your ass trying."

Jerry Rosen, Violin, 1959-1967

Jerry had just turned twenty-two when he became apprentice conductor, violinist and sometimes pianist with Cleveland. As such he was under the gun. Now, looking back, he realizes he was simply too young for the job. But Szell didn't help the situation very much. Jerry was the apprentice conductor who preceded Jimmy Levine.

Jerry was eager to tell how he got the job: "It was the only time that Szell was really nice to me. I was in my final year at Curtis where I was obligated to do only one orchestral rehearsal a week. So I spent much time in New York as a freelance musician and studying with Galamian. That winter, when the Cleveland Orchestra came to town on its February tour, my old teacher, Joseph Gingold, told me the Cleveland Orchestra was reviving its position of apprentice conductor. This position had previously been held jointly by Louis Lane and Seymour Lipkin. Joe thought I would be a natural and knew I was interested in conducting. I played the piano and it was a job for a piano player. So I decided to audition and gathered together the first movement of the 'Waldstein Sonata.' I can't imagine how I played it then because I can't play it now! I brought the violin to one of the rehearsal studios at Carnegie Hall and Joe was there with Szell. I played the piano and then the violin. I played some of the Brahms Concerto and the Bach C major Sonata, which was my big gun. Szell wrote something on a piece of manuscript paper. It was the bass line of a Bach chorale with figured bass. He asked me to harmonize the inner parts. Fortunately I loved harmony and counterpoint so I was able to do it correctly and quickly." Then he asked

Jerry who had brought the score of 'Ein Heldenleben' with him to play on the violin and to read the score at the piano. After putting him through several more hoops he finally said: "I think you will do." "That was the last time he said anything nice to me," said Jerry.

Jerry began with the orchestra the following fall in the back of the second violin section and had one opportunity to conduct that first year which was the procedure with apprentices and conducting fellows. He conducted the Prokofiev D major Violin Concerto with Danny Majeske. Szell was supportive musically when Jerry could get the courage to ask him a question. But as our interview went on, Jerry became hesitant, reluctant to continue. When he finally did, he explained that what he was going to say was still difficult for him after all these years. Evidently Szell was more concerned with the way Jerry dressed and the way he talked than with his musical skills. In retrospect Jerry admitted: "I was a little animal. I had come out of sleeping in rented rooms and eating in cheap restaurants for four years in school. I didn't know how people talked at society parties and was careless about the way I dressed. Those were all things that, if I were going to be a conductor, would have to be considered. But the way he addressed them was to roll over me with a tank which simultaneously antagonized and intimidated me. Like most people, when I am frightened that I might say the wrong thing, then very likely I will. I'm even getting nervous talking about it now."

Jerry thought I might remember what he termed the "stain on the collar" incident. This was toward the end of the first cross country tour in 1960 when the orchestra went to the west coast. Jerry had spent a good deal of time writing a violin concerto and wanted Szell to look at it. Szell finally agreed to do so when the orchestra was in Eugene, Oregon. He agreed to take Jerry to dinner and look at the score then. As Jerry described it: "That afternoon I was practicing but, bad luck, the chin rest on my violin occasionally stained my collar. This happened. I didn't have a clean shirt. When I met him at the hotel as we entered the dining room he turned and said: 'What's that on your collar?' I could feel my stomach churning. I knew something terrible was going to happen. He worked himself into a frothing rage. I must say in his defense, if I were he, I would have been distracted also, but I certainly wouldn't publicly have picked him up by the collar and shaken him like a dog."

"He did that?"

"Yes, he did. He said: 'I'll look at your score but I won't go to dinner with you. I won't go to dinner with a man who has a stain on his collar.' The point was correct but the manner was such that it took me decades to see that he had a point."

Jerry continued: "He left me standing there dumbfounded. That was the end of the season and I was going to Puerto Rico to play Festival Casals. But I had a girlfriend in New York and wanted to spend some time with her so I spent my whole week's salary on a plane ticket from Spokane to New York from whence I was going to San Juan. You guys took the train to Cleveland for two and a half days in uppers and lowers. Meanwhile at the airport, I had the great luck to run into Szell who was taking the same plane. He told me he was glad to see me and handed me a copy of a book he thought I should read: 'How to Win Friends and Influence People!'"

That reminded me of our arrival in Spokane. When we got off the train there was no transportation for the players to the hotel. There was only one taxi and, of course, Szell and Barksdale took it. I was on the curb nearby when Szell suddenly decided to be the big protector of the orchestra. Since there were no cabs he berated Barksdale in front of the orchestra. Barksdale turned down the window of the cab and called out in his Carolina accent "Room for one mowah!" All the musicians ran the opposite direction but I was too close to run so I had to join them. All the way to the hotel Szell ranted at Barksdale, seemingly for my benefit. Safe to say it was not a comfortable ride.

Jerry categorized Szell as very old European and pre-World War I Austrian. "If you were above him, he kissed your ass and if you were below him he spat on you. That was the normal way of doing things. This is really difficult to talk about but, in my opinion, he was the most explicitly anti-Semitic person I have ever met. Of course, we know he was Jewish and we know he converted."

I suggested he converted the way Mahler did, as a career move. But Jerry believed there was more to it, at least intellectually. "There was one point when I was having trouble in my personal life with a woman. I talked to him about it and his response is emblazoned on my memory: 'Get yourself a good, intelligent (I thought he was going to say therapist) priest and become a Catholic.' My jaw hit the floor. My own father, whom I loved very much, was a wonderful human being. It seemed Szell was trying to replace him. What is remarkable is though I was only around him for eight years and that was forty years ago, he is still very much a presence. He probably

112

made a bigger impact on me than any single person outside my immediate family.

"The last thing he said to me was on a summer festival tour in London in '67 when we were recording the Mozart C minor Symphony at St. John's Wood studio in London. At one of the breaks I was practicing a Bach sonata. He stopped and corrected my phrasing. 'When are you going to outgrow the vulgarity of your heritage?' he said."

I was stunned to hear this and asked Jerry if this was the only time he had made such a reference. He then vented his outrage...Szell once told him he had to become "more genteel and more gentile." In his opinion, Szell was a walking textbook of Freudian neuroses.

Suddenly Jerry changed direction and reminded me of the moment that none of us who were there will ever forget. "I was there in 1965 when Marc walked out. Every time I play the Prokofiev Fifth Symphony when we get to that passage where it happened in the third movement my heart beats a little faster." I acknowledged the same experience, how scared we all were, how we couldn't breathe each fearing that lightening bolts would strike us at any moment. Ironically, Marc had told Joe Adato that morning: "This should be an easy week." Jerry remembers how calm Szell remained while Marc was throwing a tantrum and said simply to Marc: "If you feel that way you have to leave the orchestra." Marc said: "I will," stood up, put his oboe away while muttering obscenities under his breath and was gone.

I reminded Jerry of an earlier incident of this kind. It was in a recording session in Cleveland's Masonic Auditorium. I heard a roar, some cursing and banging noises. Marc angrily slammed his oboe into its case. The orchestra was playing a serene accompaniment to what was meant to be an oboe solo. Suddenly, "Get yourself another boy." He walked right past Szell, out the hall and into the hallway. I was scared as was everyone. I thought I was going to be skinned alive just for being there. We all did, but Szell kept on conducting. Here's the orchestra playing the accompaniment to an oboe solo that was not there because the oboist had just left the scene. Joe Gingold tore out and stopped Marc just before he left the building. He said: "Marc, calm down, calm down. What would your father or mother say?" — not hopeful because Marc had problems with his father and especially his type A mother who was ever pressing him to do better. Olin Trogdon, the personnel manager found him and said: "You son of a bitch, get back in there or I'll blackball you from every orchestra in the United States." It took forty-five minutes to bring Marc back. Only he could have survived that episode but it was tough on him. Szell adored Marc but treated him worse than anyone else. So when people tell me: he was tough on some people but was "always nice to me" I know that's because expectations were different with different people.

Jerry concurred. "That was a very complicated psyche, but let's talk about good things."

Jerry told me about his experiences with other orchestras that were not as disciplined as Cleveland. When he began conducting professionally he started to appreciate Szell's methods. "He taught me my trade. He could create an esprit in the orchestra in spite of himself. A lot of the time it was united against him, but however you do it..."

Jerry praised Szell for his versatile and expressive left hand. It was Szell who opened the universe of

Mahler for Jerry but Szell had a "rather contemptuous attitude toward Mahler. Szell considered Mahler vulgar." As Jerry analyzed it: "He projected his own internal anger and conflicts onto Mahler. I could neither deal with this nor stand up to him. Only two people I knew could: Abe Skernick and Jimmy Levine. Abe once told me he was living on borrowed time. He came within inches of being killed in World War II and everything after that was a bonus. He wasn't going to be afraid of George Szell.

"Jimmy was an apprentice conducting 'Don Juan' and decided to clean up some of the string passages. I remember Szell shouting at him from out in the hall. While still conducting Jimmy turned around to face Szell and instead of turning back he did a complete 360, not stopping the beat. His whole body language was: 'give me a break.' It just didn't phase him.

Szell's expectations of his orchestra never faltered. When he heard the orchestra had misbehaved with other conductors in his absence, he berated us: "No matter who is here, play for them as if you were playing for me. Remember **you** are the **Cleveland Orchestra!**" After Szell's death, Bernstein came to do a Mahler symphony with the orchestra at Blossom. When he came to the podium we were all sitting on the edge of our seats, excited, filled with anticipation. Bernstein said: "Five rehearsals, what are we to do? You know it, I know it." Despite this the orchestra gave its all, playing fabulously but Lenny just plodded through the music routinely. In the last rehearsal it dawned on him that he was miles behind the orchestra and he began to involve himself in the music. After the concert, coming back on stage for bows, he stopped, put his arm around the shoulder of one of the violinists and said: "You guys are so-o-o fuckin' good."

After years of studying, performing and recording the "Eroica" Szell felt the necessity of rehearsing this masterpiece but on one surprising occasion Jerry recalled him saying: "Gentlemen, I think we are in pretty good shape. Let's go home." Rare occasions. Usually he said: "This is the Beethoven Fifth. We have to play it as if it were the very first performance and that no one in the audience has heard it before."

To sum up our interview, Jerry left me with these thoughts: "I learned to be a musician from Szell, Casals, and Serkin. Music was their religion. It is the thing I organized my life around, the thing that matters most to me, that offends me when it is done poorly. For hands-on nuts and bolts, he was the one. But as a musician he was one of several yet, I feel, despite all the pain he caused, I am better off having known him. We have the duty to pass this heritage on. We are the first and perhaps the last generation of American musicians to be immersed in that tradition."

Michael Goldman, Violin, 1962-1965; 1969-1973

When Szell asked Michael how his dad was doing (Michael had asked for a few days off to visit him), Michael was shocked. That act of kindness seemed so out of character for Szell who never made small talk and communicated very little with most of the players. So often one was met with stony silence even when saying good morning.

Michael told one of the popular elevator stories: It was on tour and he was going down the elevator when Bert and Joan Siegel got in. A couple of floors later, Szell joined them. "There we were, the four of us, all together, close in the elevator. We all said: 'Good morning, Mr. Szell.' Then Bert said: 'Mr. Szell, have you tried the restaurant here? It's not very good.' Szell looked at him and said: 'If you don't like it, walk out of the hotel, go around the corner and eat at a different restaurant.' Poor Bert walked into a buzz saw trying to make small talk with the 'old man.'"

Michael had two auditions. The second occurred when he wanted to play in the Mozart orchestra, which was a smaller, chamber size orchestra. This was in November and Szell set the audition for February. "So I worked my ass off. I figured I would have to play Mozart for him so I took the easiest, the G major." Michael had a recording of Stern playing it with Szell and the Cleveland. He knew Szell was a stickler for trills so he studied every trill Stern made and marked it in his part — "above, below, wherever he started it — that's where I started it. Audition time came and after I played the first movement, Szell came to the stage and said: 'Do you know how you are supposed to play the trills?' 'Yes, sir, every trill is supposed to be played from above the printed note,' I responded. 'Do you know,' he said, 'you did not play one trill accurately? Why wouldn't you start every one from above?' I said: 'Well, sometimes...melodically...' '**No**, there's no excuse, every trill from above! Play a little of the slow movement.' So I did but didn't hold a certain whole note long enough. He roared: '**Why didn't you play that note long enough? Do you know what the accompaniment is? Sing it —Sing it.**' I did. 'That's right,' he said, 'so how can you possibly not hold it long enough?' 'Well...it's an audition and there's no accompaniment so I thought...' '**No, there's no excuse, absolutely no excuse.** That will be all.' I thought it was the end of my life. The next morning on the bulletin board was a seating change which advanced me in the violin section allowing me to play in the chamber orchestra. I thought it was heaven playing in that small orchestra.

Szell seemed kinder in Michael's first audition. Szell gave Michael some second violin parts of "Ein Heldenleben" which he had never seen. He got stuck on a passage and continued to get stuck on it. Szell finally told him: "I want you to take two minutes, do whatever you need to do, then try it again." Finally Michael "limped through it and Szell said: 'That will be all.' About an hour later Szell called me into his office and said: 'You have a nice sound, you play rhythmically okay but you have no experience. You must promise me that you will work hard.' I told him that was the least I could do and he boomed out: '**What did you say?**' I repeated: 'That's the least I could do' and then he said something I'll never forget: 'You must remember that you are going to play in an orchestra the likes of which the world has never known.'"

Michael described his first rehearsal as "mind boggling. The tempos were so quick and all the bows in front of me were going in the same direction so perfectly — and to hear the woodwinds together — the intonation!! To hear the flat sound of the first trumpet — I thought, what's wrong with the trumpet player? I didn't realize after listening to a sharp trumpet player in El Paso for many years that his intonation was wrong. Bernie's playing was wonderful. I remember Marc Lifschey. He was the soul of the orchestra. I got chills up and down my spine when he played."

The most memorable tour for Michael was the tour to the Soviet Union and playing in the white marble hall in Leningrad. "In one box sat Oistrach, Rostropovich and Kogan, all the big guys." I, too, can still picture Khatchaturian and Shostakovich among others sitting in the boxes in Moscow.

Playing in Carnegie Hall, Michael recalled Beverly Sills singing Mozart's "Exultate Jubilate" with the orchestra. "She had that long flowing red hair and a Kelly green dress. She was a sight and sang the hell out of that piece. When she left the stage I was one of the first to follow her. Her husband was there and she slapped him on the back and said: 'I got every damn note.'"

One of Michael's vivid memories was on Szell's last tour in Tokyo when we played the overture to 'The Bartered Bride.' "The second violins have an important solo which was always very clean but in rehearsal it was getting messy and it was the last time we were going to rehearse it. At intermission Szell called a meeting of the second violin section in his dressing room and said: 'The

119

Bartered Bride. We are approaching disaster. I only want four stands up until letter C.' I was on the fourth stand and I thought: this better be really clean or he'll think it was us. It was clean and I was happy it was over."

We both recalled when Szell would turn to the basses in the "Eroica" during the "Marche Funebre." He would take a second, turn, face the basses and stab that note, a low A flat. It was terrifying and at the same time, one of the great moments in all music. We continued to talk about Szell's special skills as a conductor and interpreter of great music. Michael said he played the Sibelius Second many times since leaving Cleveland "but nobody could achieve that final climax like Szell. Every conductor would blow himself out early but somehow Szell held the reins taut and wouldn't let the orchestra go until the very end. Then it would just blossom. He had great timing in many pieces for which he was not famous. He was an inner voice conductor. He spent a lot of time on violas and the seconds. He wanted accompaniment right and the bow stroke correct. In the famous New Yorker article about him in the sixties, he expressed concern as to how to keep everyone alert and involved in the music at all times. That, and clarity, were important to him. The dotted 8th/16th was the whole spirit of that orchestra. In rehearsal, to his dying day, he would use the thick end of his stick on his music stand to illustrate the articulation he had to have. It's impossible to do that correctly without counting it in your mind. Rhythmic subdivision was the key. It was his way or the highway."

Allen Kofsky, Trombone, 1961-2000

In 1950 Allen was called to be a replacement for an orchestra trombonist who would be out for a length of time. Szell was in New York at the time and told the personnel manager (Olin Trogdon) that he would bring someone back from New York but Trogdon prevailed upon him to give Allen a chance. When Szell returned to Cleveland, he summoned Allen to his office. "I was too naive to be nervous. Szell asked: 'What are you doing now?' But before I could tell him, he told me that I was in the construction business with my father. He already knew everything. It was a rhetorical question. Then he said: 'How do you stay in shape? You play a brass instrument.' I said: I play musical shows at the Hanna Theater here. He was satisfied."

In 1956 the general manager asked Allen to sign a contract to play the European tour the following spring. Allen was not comfortable for two reasons: he might be needed in the construction business and he might have to cover for the tuba player on the trombone if necessary which he didn't want to do. Nonetheless, he signed an agreement with an escape clause and went on tour. In 1959 he replaced the ailing trombonist again. "During that season I was told that the Board of Trustees had allowed Mr. Szell to hire another trombonist so that was my audition, from 1955 to 1961!!"

One day Szell asked Allen if he played the bass trumpet. "Yes," he said, "but there are very few things that call for it." Szell was outraged and replied: "I know that. Don't tell me! We're going to do the Janacek Sinfonietta which calls for two bass trumpets but we'll use one." Allen said he didn't have a bass trumpet but

Szell assured him the orchestra had one. The same thing happened one time when Szell asked him to play the tenor tuba. Of course, the orchestra **had** one! After the first rehearsal, Szell called him in and said: "I've never conducted that using the tenor tuba." He actually liked it better on the tenor tuba than on the customary Wagner tuba. I guess that was a compliment.

Allen, too, had an elevator story. But this time he was in the hotel lobby, not on the elevator. "The nearby elevator door opened to reveal Szell, Peg Glove (his secretary) and Bill Martin (the general manager). "I heard an explosion of language. Szell was using all kinds of vulgarities and four letter words. That was the end of Bill Martin! who went on to head the Brooklyn Academy of Music."

Allen recalled an incident when Szell got angry with him for changing instruments. Szell required everyone in the trombone section to play an instrument built by the Conn Instrument factory. They were beautiful sounding instruments but the slide was difficult to move. Allen knew of a Cleveland company that made very good trombones. They offered to make one for him because it would be good advertising for them. "I told them it had to be exactly like the one I was playing, same color, same laquer, because Szell had visual hearing. When he saw something, he thought he heard it. I told them I would not tell a soul about this and they were to say nothing. They agreed to make the horn and I used it successfully for about six months. Szell, it seemed, never knew, but one morning he asked to see me with my trombone. When I walked in, the manager was there too.

Szell said to me: "I understand that you are playing on a different instrument."

I didn't know what to say. I told him I'd been playing it for quite a while.

"Why did you change without my permission?" he asked, glaring at me. "Contractually you are to be playing the instrument I tell you to play!"

Unhesitatingly I protested: "That trombone is terrible. I tried to talk to you about it but you always turned away. Has there been something wrong with the sound?"

"No," he said. "I didn't notice anything wrong but somebody told me you are playing a different horn."

Szell pounded on his desk, yelled, screamed and had a tantrum. I thought I was finished and done for. He then issued the following instruction: "Tomorrow morning bring the trombone you played for the Sibelius Second a couple of weeks ago."

"This IS the trombone I played it on, this new one," I insisted.

But he was adamant, so the next morning I carried both instruments to the stage and played the Tannhauser Overture on both instruments.

"Hmph, they do sound similar. Play the introduction to Act III of 'Lohengrin.'"

I did on both instruments. Then I played the Sibelius on both and he said: "You know, they are not only similar, they are identical." "That was what I was trying to tell you," I said and he replied, "Yes, but it was **still** without my knowledge."

Elmer Setzer, Violin, 1949-1990
Marie Setzer, Violin, 1961-1990

Elmer and Marie had retired some years back. By the time I interviewed them, they were both in frail health so we just renewed our friendship and wished each other well. Before we hung up Marie said: "You are sort of at a distance from it after a while. You look back and it's something in the beginning that you just want to forget about. But now that we don't play any more we think about what fantastic concerts they were. It's a different story."

Richard Wiener, Percussion, 1963-2013

When Richard was a percussion student at Indiana University his teacher obtained a couple of interviews for him, one of which was in Cleveland. In preparation for that audition, twenty-three year old Richard started listening to recordings of the Cleveland Orchestra, considered one of the big five. During that time Szell appeared on the cover of Time Magazine and was compared to Vince Lombardi in the cover article. It was 1962. Famous orchestras had been invited to open Avery Fisher Hall and Cleveland was among them. Comparisons were inevitable. Critics declared Cleveland the best orchestra in the land. Time Magazine portrayed Szell as a tough taskmaster but one who knew how to achieve his artistic ideals.

Richard practiced hard for the audition. When the time came, Cloyd Duff, the orchestra's tympanist, was on stage; Szell and Louis Lane were in the hall. Richard was center stage near the footlights. As he describes it: "They actually talked to me. Well, not exactly. Szell didn't talk to me. He talked to Cloyd as if I weren't in the room. After I played all the standard stuff, snare drums, cymbals, xylophone, bells and tympani, Szell said to Cloyd: 'Have him play something on the castanets.' The first thing I thought of was the castanet part in Carmen. My adrenalin was really pumping so I played it too fast. I kept thinking: they can see my legs shaking. Szell said: 'Too fast. Watch.' He conducted and I played along with him. My audition was over."

Richard's first rehearsal was the following September. The first thing he played was the tambourine in Berlioz' Roman Carnival Overture, one of Szell's signature pieces. "I was a nervous wreck playing tambourine, which, except for the cymbals, is the most exposed percussion part. Szell walked on stage, said 'Good morning, gentlemen, nice to see you back, let's get to work' all in one breath. Amazing! Later, during the allegro I miscounted, coming in early because I was so nervous. But when I looked up Szell had a smile on his face. He never said a word to me. During the entire rehearsal I was transfixed by what he was doing up there."

Richard recalled that at the end of a Wagner or Strauss piece there was a single triangle note. Szell called him over and said: "When this note happens the heavens must open up. You must lift, lift, lift. See me at intermission." At intermission Szell took Richard's triangle and beater. He struck the triangle and held the beater on too long making a clunking sound and said: "Now you do it." "I did it correctly lifting quickly and high. That's what he wanted. It was a visual thing. The lift occurs in a microsecond — the rest of the lift is for the audience." Szell then wanted to hear several triangles to pick just the right one for this particular note. "We returned to the stage where I had eight or ten triangles to play for him. After I hit several he said: "I need to hear this out in the hall" and left the stage. The rest of the section and I were left standing and waiting but he never came back. So we chose the best sounding triangle and he seemed content."

However, Szell continued to bug Richard about lifting. Exasperated, Richard told his wife: "If he says one more word about this triangle I'm going to tell him to shove it." Instead, Richard decided to stare him down during that night's performance. "I kept looking at him,

126

staring him down, getting ready to play the triangle note. Right before that moment, he turned away and looked at another section. I played the note and that was it. He sensed enough was enough. He was an absolute bully."

Cloyd asked the section to decide how the parts were shared. Aside from the cymbals played by the great Emil Sholle, all other parts were up for grabs. Along with Emil and Cloyd, Richard, Bob Matson and Joe Adato comprised the percussion section. The Bartok Concerto was scheduled to be performed in '63 and '64. When the time came to decide who was to play the infamous snare drum part, no one wanted it, so it was left to Richard, the "new guy." Richard played it and everything was fine. However, when the orchestra recorded the Bartok, Szell changed the drum part in the chorale of the second movement — he altered at least one of the rhythms. As Richard tells it: "Every score I had ever seen was different than what he insisted I play." Knowing this was to be recorded I asked him about the correction. He explained that Bartok himself had corrected the part. So that's the way we recorded it. Later, before we took this piece on tour, he said to me: "Deek, I discovered a mistake in the Bartok. This has to be changed." So he returned it to the original notation. As a result, for the next forty years people have asked me why I played a different rhythm than what is printed in the score..."

Richard, too, had an elevator story: "I got on the elevator and Szell started going through the Bartok from the first measure of the first movement, every measure, every note and how he wanted me to shape it. This was before a Carnegie Hall tour and, of course, he was manic. When we got to the ground floor he said: 'Well, all in all, it is very good. Don't change a thing.'

"When Emil retired from our section, Szell called Cloyd, Louis and me into his room and said: 'We're going to have a percussion audition. As you know, I don't have much use for percussion (he meant in his repertoire). I would like you three to run the audition.' I remember Cloyd or Louis saying: 'Suppose you don't like whom we choose?' 'Well,' he said, 'then I'll fire all three of you. Harr, harr, harr.'"

Bernard Adelstein, Trumpet, 1960-1988

Bernie had given much thought to what he wanted to say about Szell and the orchestra. He began talking about his audition in Severance Hall in the old broadcasting room. Bernie played and Szell offered him the job. "I signed a two year contract with one of his famous one-way options. If he wanted you, you had to stay and if he didn't, you were out."

Bernie talked about playing the Walton Second Symphony on tour. I reminded him that we recorded it. It was a great recording. He then referred to a small passage toward the end of the symphony: "I thought there was an error in my part. For a while I was in unison with the violins, but one spot just didn't seem to match. I went to Szell's office with that part and showed it to him. He had a small console piano and without even looking at the piano, with my part in one hand, he started to play the whole score with his other hand explaining to me why it was correct and written that way. He knew every note in the whole piece. It was very impressive."

Another story had to do with Leon Fleisher, a Szell favorite, who was often a piano soloist with the orchestra. It was on tour and he was playing the "Emperor Concerto." Before we got to New York, Bernie recalls, Leon was having a bit of trouble with one run. "I got to the hall early that night and heard someone practicing the problem run. As I listened I thought, oh, boy, he's got it perfect. I walked in the back of the hall and there was Fleisher standing by the piano. Szell was playing. It was absolutely perfect."

As so many of us, Bernie was astounded by the orchestra's sound and perfection. "In my first rehearsal, I just couldn't imagine how that could happen. It was breathtaking. Little by little he disassembled the score and little by little he put it together. By Thursday morning it was in his image just the way he wanted. I told my wife: 'I can't believe how perfectly the orchestra played and they called it a **rehearsal!**'"

Bernie told me about his experience in Paris when the whole trumpet section was instructed by Szell on their day off to go to a factory that made authentic coronets. Some pieces of Berlioz and Cesar Franck were written for cornets as well as trumpets. Most orchestras just used trumpets but Szell wanted to differentiate between the sound of the trumpets and cornets. "So he made an appointment at the factory, gave us the address and told us to meet him at nine in the morning. As you can imagine, we were not too happy about this. The whole trumpet section hailed a cab and arrived at the factory twenty minutes early. We didn't know what to do with the time so we each wandered off in a different direction. There were four of us including David Zauder, Tom Wohlwender, Dick Smith and myself. Exactly at nine we converged as Szell arrived by taxi. He saw the four of us coming from different streets and said: **Now that is what I call Cleveland Orchestra precision.**

String articulation in Cleveland was so incisive and unique that it became the hallmark of the orchestra. Bernie played in Minnesota before Cleveland and explained that there it was a bit different. "Dorati used to like the articulation very short and crisp, but Szell wanted it even shorter. The shortest note had to be given a little extra energy with silence on either side so it would not get muddled or lost. While recording the "Firebird" Szell wanted certain notes emphasized this way. I said: 'I am playing them quite short.' He said: 'No, no, no. I want every note cut off with your tongue.' This is a real no, no. It causes ugly sounds like a chicken farm. So I said: 'I hate to play that way,' and he said: 'That's exactly what I want. Every note must sound like an arrow piercing the heart.' I really hated to play like that but we did it and during the recording he looked up and smiled."

Lynn Harrell, Cello, 1963-1970

When I spoke to Lynn, he had just seen the DVD of the Bell Telephone Hour broadcast praising George Szell and the Cleveland Orchestra. "Great to hear Szell say again what was like a broken record to us. Great to hear those words. Wow! He was so right."

Lynn was in the orchestra from 1963 to the end of the Blossom Festival season of 1970, the year Szell died. He had come to Cleveland to see Robert Shaw who had made a recording of Bach cantatas with Lynn's father, Mack Harrell. Robert Shaw was Lynn's godfather. "Bob had been very close to both my parents. My mother had died as the result of a car accident in November and this was around Christmas time." Shaw encouraged Lynn to play for Szell. "So George Silfes, a clarinetist with the orchestra, played piano for me. I played the whole Beethoven A major Sonata. Then I played the second movement of the Dvorak Concerto. I finished both pieces and there was much talk and fuss over George just being able to sit down and play those pieces. But they didn't make any fuss over me at all. Szell did point out that I had played a wrong note in the Dvorak. It was actually published wrong in the score.

"The night before this experience Shaw had introduced me to Szell who said: 'I've heard so much about you. I'm bound to be disappointed when I hear you play.' Catching him quite off guard, I smiled and said: 'You probably will be disappointed, Mr. Szell.' Not a propitious start to an audition. But I was in town and Szell did talk about working at the Met with my dad so he decided to spend a little time listening to me play. A

132

month or two later I received a letter from Beverly Barksdale offering me a job.

"Leonard Rose had suggested to me that there were two ways to build a solo career. One was to win a contest and I had already tried that — at the Moscow Second International Tchaikovsky Competition — got to the semifinals. The other, which appealed to me, was to join a great orchestra as Rose had done. So I joined the orchestra and my life began.

"It never occurred to me how to prepare for an orchestra, about following the conductor, about learning the music. The Sibelius Second Symphony was on the first concerts of the season. The piece suddenly began and just as suddenly I was three bars behind!"

Lynn and Diane Mather both joined the cello section the same year and both were nervous. But Diane had more orchestra experience than Lynn. She had played in the Curtis Orchestra as a student while Lynn was preparing for a solo career.

I reminded Lynn of the time he and I were talking backstage when suddenly Szell appeared. With urgency, he called to Lynn and asked: "Do you know the solo from the Second Brahms Piano Concerto?" I overheard Lynn reply that he'd heard it but never played it. Szell said to Lynn: "Learn it because next year you'll be playing it and recording it." That was the first hint that he was considering Lynn for principal. But something happened during the first half of the program. At intermission he beckoned Lynn again and took it all back. "You'll never be principal."

Lynn corrected my facts a bit. All this evidently occurred after Lynn had already signed a contract. "During the concert he kept staring at me. At intermission he said: 'I've changed my mind. You are not mature enough.' I knew the music by memory, I thought I was playing quite well, but he wanted the contract back. Harry Fuchs asked me what happened because I was in tears. I told him that Szell wanted the contract back that I had just signed the day before appointing me principal. Fuchs said: 'You don't have to return it. That contract is binding.' So I went back to Szell the next night and said: 'Mr. Szell, I think you are acting precipitously. I feel I am ready to be principal and I'm not giving you the contract back.' Shit hit the fan and my life was made impossible.

"Szell told me privately backstage that I would never be principal, that I would sit at the back of the section, not on third stand. I would collect my contractual money that I had negotiated for principal but I would never sit up there. Then he called me in five minutes before the first rehearsal of the following season, 1966, and said: 'We're going to see if you can handle the responsibilities of being principal. You will alternate with Jerry Appleman every other week. You'll start as principal this week. As you know, we're doing the Mahler Fourth and we're recording it on Friday. Good luck.'" The recording session went well as did the alternating principal position. Lynn said he learned a lot that year. Much was starting to rub off not only of Szell's musicianship and way of striving to become a better musician and interpreter, but also Jimmy Levine's work at the Cleveland Institute of Music which inspired him.

When I asked Lynn about his first rehearsal, he, like so many of us, was "just blown away, there was so much sonority, so much tone. Szell was careful in choosing players who were bright and had a deep interest in the overall musical product rather than just in their

134

own careers. He knew how to talk to the musicians and involve them at a very high level in the intricacies of listening and adjusting to their colleagues." The DVD Lynn had mentioned at the beginning of the interview reminded him how different Szell was from other conductors. "Others look at the score and criticize but they are looking at the score. They don't look at the players and it seems to be more about them than about the music or criticism. It wasn't that way for Szell. It was about trying to get the musicians to make the music better."

By the time Lynn was to sign another three-year contract, Jerry Appleman had accepted a position with the New York Philharmonic. So the principal position went to Lynn. As part of his new contractual agreement Lynn asked to play a concerto with the orchestra at Carnegie Hall. Szell agreed to the Schumann and Dvorak concertos, one of which would be in New York. He started working with Lynn about ten months before the performance. "While he was listening to me play, he was playing the orchestra part from the score at the piano as he loved to do. He didn't like piano reductions. We worked on the Schumann Concerto and I played it in Cleveland. At each orchestra rehearsal he insisted I play the entire concerto through to the end. By concert time I was exhausted and quaking in my boots, worse than I had ever been in my whole life. After performing in Cleveland, we played it at Carnegie Hall. Some time after the tour, Szell asked me to play through the Dvorak Concerto with him. When he was criticizing he'd say: 'You can't play freely there because the orchestra has to come in precisely in tempo.' But his tone of voice implied that if you knew the score, if you were born in Prague, you would know these things, but you don't, because you are a stupid American kid.

"It was awful the way he treated people. Deep down, I think, he just wanted the music to be better. When he told me this, I argued with him: 'I can be free those first two beats. The orchestra doesn't have anything to play. The orchestra comes in after the third beat and I know you will give a very strong beat to the right demonstrating the third beat. Therefore I can play freely!!' **Long Silence**. I mean like thirty seconds. His facial expression was changing somewhat and he was staring at the score. Then he said: 'Okay, let's try again from the beginning.' About a week later I got a note to appear in his office and he said: 'Unfortunately there is no space for you to play the Dvorak Concerto with me next year. So what I suggest is that we continue to work on it. Then you play it with Louis on one of the runout concerts. The year after you can play it with me.'

"I knew why he was doing this. He wanted me to sign another three-year contract the third year of my existing contract, which would keep me in the orchestra for two more years. I could see through his plan because he was being so sacchariney and nice. I said: 'Okay, I'll play it with Louis' but I made no commitment for the following year. So that was the last I worked on the Dvorak Concerto with him."

Jorge Sicre, Cello, 1961-1991

Jorge decided right away that he had no stories to tell and nothing to say. I told him this book was not intended to be a hagiography — all of us on bent knee at the foot of George Szell. This must have encouraged him because his next words were: "He was a son of a bitch. He was a bastard." But then came the qualifier that I got from so many of those I interviewed: "Although I had no problem with him. He liked me. I'd give him his way."

Jorge's audition story was interesting. He had left Cuba when "the bearded wonder took office" and arrived in Miami, Florida with his wife and three year old son on one of the last legal flights. "I didn't have to go on the boat," he told me. "If I did I would probably still be in Cuba because I'm a coward." He played freelance jobs but was basically in limbo because, not being a citizen, he wasn't allowed to join the union.

"One day I got a phone call at an outdoor phone booth because we didn't have a phone. It was Trogdon who said: 'Your teacher,' meaning Leonard Rose, 'was just extolling your virtues as a cellist to the "boss." He needs one more cellist to complete the section and wants you to audition.' I immediately responded that I couldn't afford the trip. He replied: 'Don't worry, we'll send you and your family a ticket. You can stay for a month or two and see if you like it. If you don't, no questions asked.'

"When I got to Cleveland I began rehearsing with the orchestra. I was on a sort of probation and hadn't played for him but his coke bottle eyes were on me the whole time. Eventually Szell wanted to hear me and the audition went well. I was offered the job."

Jorge was thrilled because he had always admired Szell and the Cleveland Orchestra. He began cello studies in Havana at age twelve and his good friend was the son of the principal cellist in the Havana Philharmonic. They loved to play a recording of the Dvorak with Casals and the Prague Philharmonic. "They played like gods, absolutely gorgeous together. The recording was from 1938 and Szell was conducting."

I asked Jorge about his first rehearsal. "I was shaking like a leaf. Don't forget I wasn't in the orchestra yet. I didn't have a contract. It was sort of a live audition. I felt like the whole world was looking at me. And that was the orchestra at its peak. Marc Lifschey was there, Myron Bloom, Marcellus, Sharp, Goslee, all the stars. I flipped out."

Jorge played in the Severance String Quartet with three other orchestra members. They invited Szell to one of their performances. He asked what they were playing. Jorge told him that among other things was the big E flat, Op. 127 quartet of Beethoven. "He said: 'Oh, that's a wonderful piece but the scherzo is a mazurka. Don't play it too fast.' He had the piece in his head!"

On the last tour, Japan, 1970, Szell told Jorge he wanted to talk to him on the plane. This, of course, caused immediate anxiety. When he saw him, Szell said: "What is going on with you and your stand partner?" Jorge then used some negatively descriptive words about his partner. "Szell tried not to put me in a bad position talking about my colleague. He took off his glasses like he used to, started polishing them and said: 'Jorge, you really can't stand him, can you?' I said: 'No, Maestro, I can't.' 'Okay,' he said. That was the last time we talked." This became a furious feud. Eventually Jorge's stand partner asked Louis Lane to move Jorge back in the section. Instead Louis moved the stand partner back. When Szell heard about this, he understood.

For Jorge, the highlight of the season was the Carnegie Hall tour. "Severance is okay but when you played the bottom of the instrument at Carnegie Hall there was no end to it. It all sounded so gorgeous." He noted how tense Szell was at Carnegie Hall which reminded us both of a speech he made to the orchestra: "Gentlemen," he said. "This is Carnegie Hall. So what!"

Jorge witnessed a scene in Lucerne, Switzerland. Szell was knocking on Karajan's dressing room door. Karajan opened it but before Szell could say a word, Karajan said: "Not now, George" and slammed the door in his face. Jorge, of course, pretended to see none of this. I remember what a master Karajan was. He lived up to his superlative reputation. His was a special presence.

The last story Jorge shared with me was about a retirement party for violinist Sol Fiore with Joe Gingold as master of ceremonies. Szell was fond of breathy multiple up bows in quiet accompanying passages. Sol made it known he was not fond of playing them. So for Sol's party Joe had a bow made with two heads and when Szell saw it, he asked: "What kind of bow has two heads?" "Maestro," replied Sol, "it only plays up bow no matter what you do."

Thomas Wohlwender, Trumpet, 1960-1971

For his audition, Tom walked on stage with three instruments in his arms and a mute or two. To his surprise Szell was on stage and wanted to shake hands. "I didn't have any hands available. He came so close...the face, the glasses, the intensity, and the way he spoke!! He told me to play for him...."

The often-mentioned Bartok Concerto was during Tom's first year. He thought he had played his part well but Szell stopped the orchestra and said: "I can't hear the short notes." Three or four months of intense problems ensued because of those three little notes. "He couldn't hear them," Tom explained, "because Bernie's part was in a higher register. Mine was much lower in a more muddled area. That led from one thing to another and he kept going over it. A couple of times Bernie muttered under his breath: 'Jesus, get off Tom's back. This is ridiculous.' So finally one morning I came to work early and went directly to Szell's studio. I asked to play for him to prove I could play the passage. He sat down at the piano and played the seventeen bars preceding the solo. I played it. He said: 'It's perfect. That's wonderful.' And I said: 'Well???' He put his arm around me and said: 'Tom, I think we made a mountain out of a molehill.' **'We???** ' As I was going down the stairs along came Marc Lifschey who said: 'I thought I was losing my mind. Walking down the street from my apartment I heard that damn Bartok second trumpet part coming out of Severance Hall — all by itself.'"

Tom thought Szell never missed a thing. He knew all. "Once while I was warming up backstage in New York, he came over and said: 'Thomas, do you know the fake fingering for a low C sharp on your trumpet? You know, the low C sharp that is so out of tune?' My mind was going a hundred miles an hour. 'No, no.' I thought: damn he's figured out a fake fingering for the C sharp. And lo and behold, it's the only time I ever won. I said: 'No, sir, I really don't. I've played the horn for a lot of years but I don't know one. Do you?' He said: 'No, I don't,' and walked away."

One day Szell called Tom and Bernie Adelstein into his office to complain that they were using fake double-tonguing and were not to do that again. "We said we had to do that but Szell said: 'No, you can't do that in my orchestra. Use the metronome all summer and speed up your tongue.' So we both worked and worked all summer. From then on we seldom needed to double tongue. He knew that we could do it but how the hell did he know all that about the trumpet?"

Tom recalled a time at Carnegie Hall when Szell said: 'Thomas, we're going to do the Bartok on Monday evening but I don't want you to worry about it.' "That's all he needed to say. I was ready to get sick. I told him I was going to practice and pray. I remember distinctly his reply: 'Make sure you do a lot more practicing than praying.'"

Tom told me that the trumpets were always in trouble with the guest conductors so I asked him who had given Georges Prêtre the finger. "That was I. Well, I really gave him the arm. He was picking on us. Prêtre said in his French accented English: 'I am a Black Belt in karate and in my country I would "keeel" for that.'" A flaming moment in Cleveland Orchestra history!

Tom remembered nostalgically when he and other students at Curtis would stay up late listening to recordings of the Cleveland Orchestra with Szell. "I always wanted to play with that orchestra. Before Marc left it was probably the greatest orchestra that was ever assembled, chair for chair."

I need to stress that Tom said "before Marc left" because I, too, felt that was a real line drawn in the sand of history. Tom admitted he had good skills on the trumpet before coming to Cleveland "but I didn't even know how to **SPELL** the word 'ensemble' until I worked with Szell. I didn't get beyond the trumpet and become a musician until I worked with George Szell.'"

Gary Tischkoff, Violin, 1966-2009
Felix Kraus, Oboe, English Horn, 1963-2004
Alvaro DeGranda, Violin, 1966-2006

Gary: My audition wasn't bad at all. I had gotten over my nerves a week before when I auditioned in Pittsburgh. When I came to Cleveland I was fine and was hired. I remember my first rehearsal. The sound was so stunning, so amazing.

Felix: For me the big story was that, like everyone else, I felt he was looking at me constantly with those eyes!!!

Larry: Cyclops!

Felix: Yes, but he had two of them. This was a time of horn-rimmed glasses and that's what I wore. I discovered if I let them slide a bit, the rims allowed me to look at his face without seeing his eyes. I saw what I needed to see and I thought it was great. But two days later, Trogdon told me that Mr. Szell wanted to see me in his office. When I walked in he said: "Mr. Kraus, I must see your eyes. Here is the address of my optometrist. Go get your glasses fixed."

Larry: You must have been nervous when he called you in.

Felix: I was certainly **interested**. I didn't yet understand there was no right or wrong, only Szell's way in all matters. Early, perhaps the second week, we played the "Jupiter" Symphony. Mozart often doubles the first violins with the first oboe and second oboe with the second violins. My part had an awkward page turn in the last movement and since the second fiddles were playing, what the hell, I dropped a few notes. Szell was on me like a shot. I don't know whether he heard me but certainly he saw me.

Alvaro: Szell was always tense before the New York concerts. One time in rehearsal he was picking on people so much that we all agreed not to play the second half of the rehearsal in protest. Abe Skernick informed Szell. When Szell actually saw us seated in the auditorium he couldn't believe we had confronted him. We demanded an apology but he did not give a real apology, only more or less.

Larry: Marty Flowerman told me that Szell started to apologize, then said something like: "If you would only control your bad behavior, I wouldn't have to do this." Then he smiled sweetly and said: "Will that suffice?" Bert Siegel recalled him saying: "If I have offended anybody you must remember it is all for the sake of music."

Felix: A curious thing about Szell and Felix Freilich: Szell used to take the overnight train from Berlin to Prague to conduct the orchestra. Felix was a student playing in the Prague Orchestra. Much later Felix joined Cleveland and Szell never once acknowledged their having seen each other in the past. It was as if it never happened.

Larry: Why do you think that was so? Was he uncomfortable with his past?

Felix: Perhaps. One of the weirdest episodes for me was going to his memorial service in the chapel of the Catholic Church at John Carroll University.

Larry: I have heard that he was quite devout. Someone said he knew the liturgy in Latin better than any priest.

Gary: How would you like confessing to that guy?

Larry: He rode rough over a lot of us and wanted to mold every aspect of our lives.

Alvaro: I think he picked on a lot of people whom he respected. I remember Jimmy Levine conducting Strauss and Szell picking on him. The same with Lynn Harrell. Every other line he would stop and pick on him. There were passages in "La Mer" that we would mark with dashes to show how many times we repeated them in rehearsal.

Larry: Szell was not without compassion. He kept a few elderly immigrant musicians in his orchestra longer than perhaps he should because they needed a salary and back then there were no pensions. Mr. Gans was almost deaf. He sat with Ed Ormond and sometimes he would ask Ormond: "what did he say?" Despite his hearing handicap Gans knew the music and the orchestra routine very well, so he didn't get in the way. His main claim to fame, a very sweet man, was that he had actually slept with the same woman as Brahms.

Felix: Dick Smith was eating in a restaurant in Salzburg some distance from the hotel in order to have peace and quiet. Who should also be eating there but none other than Szell. When it came time for Dick to order, the waiter said: "No, no, no, your food has already been ordered." When it was time for the check, it arrived at Dick's table. It seemed that Szell was concerned with what Dick ate so it would not upset his playing, but he wasn't interested in paying for it.

Larry: Szell was increasingly being criticized for playing the same composers all the time...Schumann, Beethoven, Mozart. Wisely he looked about the world and found the brilliant young composer/conductor, Pierre Boulez, who brought more modern music to the Cleveland audience than they had ever hoped to hear. As Ed Ormond noted: "His musical interests seemed to begin where Szell's left off." Earlier Szell wanted to do the "Missa Solemnis," the Mozart Requiem and a few other choral masterpieces in Carnegie Hall but the Cleveland Orchestra chorus was not distinguished. So he hired the fabulous young choral director, Robert Shaw. He told him: I'll teach you how to conduct an orchestra; you'll build me a great chorus.

I remember the orchestra flying to Vienna in three planes. If Szell was in the third plane, we had to circle the airport so that his would be the first to land.

Felix: Yes, most people preferred to be on the plane with him because if it went down he would just point up! He would never allow it to crash.

Larry: So true. Do you remember anything about his wife, Helene?

Alvaro: One time in Lucerne at the Palace Hotel, we had a reception with a big spread. Szell pushed himself to the front of the line to get some pastries. His wife was three or four people behind him. As he started to put pastry on his plate his wife glared at him and said in a loud voice: "**George!**" He dropped the plate and it broke.

Gary: I heard a story about the newspaper boy who went to collect his bill from Szell. He knocked loud, then louder until the door opened. Szell shouted: "Don't you see the door is closed?" And the kid said: "Listen, I got a job to do too." Szell paid him.

Felix: We all seem to agree Szell was fearsome. On one occasion when I was closeted with him I felt brave enough to suggest that if he were more encouraging and smiled occasionally the results, at least for me, would be better. I suppose I felt comfortable saying that because he had been decent recently. He didn't respond and the interview soon ended. But at the next rehearsal he flashed this totally phony **smile** at me, a monster smile.

I have in more recent years had an interesting experience I would like to share. While working on the compilation of the 75th anniversary CD set, I listened once again to Szell's marvelous performance of Prokofiev's Classical Symphony and discovered one "smudge" in one of the wind player's parts. As I wanted to include this recording in the set, I wanted perfection because that is what Szell was all about. However, I discovered another performance of it with Szell at Blossom recorded about nine months later. These recordings were done many years ago and one could edit much less easily than today. Tempos had to match. At

Severance one could use any of the three concerts but it was difficult to go from the ambience of Severance Hall and its performances to that of Blossom in order to do a crossfade. Everything had to be in sync. Lo and behold the Blossom and Severance performances were in sync to within thirty seconds for half a bar. It was actually one note — so crossfade could be done without any noticeable difference. Over the span of a nine month period he had precisely the same tempo.

Bert Siegel, Violin, 1965-1995
Joan Siegel, Violin, 1965-1995
Ed Ormond, Viola, 1959-1997

Bert: When Szell invited us to join the orchestra he said: "It doesn't matter where you sit in an orchestra of this caliber." So I didn't pay too much attention. The first day of our first rehearsal I met him as he came out of his dressing room. He said: "Mr. Siegel, I must apologize for where you are sitting. It was the best I could do to keep peace in the family." This was the kindest thing I ever experienced from him.

Ed: When I arrived I was placed on the fifth stand where I sat with Isaac Gans. Right away Isaac told me he was completely deaf in one ear. The next year I was moved to the outside second stand where Laszlo Krausz was sitting. He was moved to the inside and he took this very dimly. "I know it's not your fault. It's **him**!" We became friends.

Joan: We were recording all the Beethoven concerti with the great Emil Gilels over a period of days. One day as I was walking up the stairs I was joined by Gilels who said to me: "He's not a very nice man."

Bert: I remember when Milstein came to do the Lalo Concerto. During rehearsal Milstein asked Szell if the orchestra could play a little softer. Szell said: "We'd be happy to accommodate to your small tone."

Joan: The week before Milstein arrived we were already rehearsing the Lalo.

Bert: Oh, yes. We had to know it perfectly because one never knows what an artist will do! He really didn't like musicians of Milstein's temperament.

Larry: With artists such as Casadesus, we would rehearse for five or ten minutes a day for three or four weeks ahead of time. By the time of the initial rehearsal, the quality of orchestral playing surprised and often shocked the soloists, challenging them to raise the artistic level of their own performances.

Bert: I could understand it with a concerto like Lalo which we didn't play often but he worried about so many details that would always fall into place once the soloist arrived.

Larry: Do you remember the Glenn Gould incident? Gould had already made his name with his recording of the "Goldberg Variations" and everyone was eager to work with him. He came out in a drab head to floor length coat, wearing gloves with a scarf wrapped around his throat. Everyone else was in shirt sleeves. Szell was prepared to give the downbeat for a Beethoven Concerto when Gould started to fuss with his artist's bench making it lower because he played with his hands up very high. Down and down it went with frequent stops for testing. This went on and on as Szell's frustration and impatience grew. Gould was still wearing his muffler, gloves and coat when a thoroughly aggravated Szell said: "Perhaps it might help if we cut two or three inches off your ass!"

Bert: Once we were recording an album of Rossini overtures and during the last session everything that could go wrong, did. All kinds of crazy accidents, a pencil falling during a take, music slipping off the stand, people coughing or sneezing...we did take after take. Szell liked to use the vernacular terms. When a take was acceptable, the engineer would say: "It's in the can." Szell never quite got it right. He would always say: "It's in the bag." This time after take, retake, oh, god, what an afternoon that was, he finally came back, and like everyone else he was really tired, and said: "Well, everything is fine. It's in various and sundry bags."

There were many travel stories about Szell. One happened early in our careers when the orchestra was on a western tour. We were boarding a charter plane in Phoenix. You know how they often have "elevator music" going. We were sitting close to the front and overheard Szell say to the stewardess: "Must we have that music?" She said to everyone who was in earshot: "Can you imagine, that man doesn't like music!"

Larry: Bert, you were always active in orchestra/union contract matters. I'm sure we all remember Fred Funkhouser. He was the consummate gentleman. At a meeting with the union, orchestra members wanted to change the by-laws to insure the fundamental right to ratify or not ratify any contract proposal between the union and the orchestra management. Union leaders said: "You draw up a resolution and we'll put it in the union paper for three months running and then we'll vote on it democratically." So we did, and, of course, they brought in 2500 people and voted our one hundred votes down. At one hot, stormy angry session, Fred, in a quavering voice, got the president's attention long enough to say: "But sir, sir, you're not following Robert's

Rules of Order." "I'm Robert's Rules of Order here," he replied. "Now **you** sit down and shut up." Our relationship with the union was at the lowest possible ebb.

Emilio Llinas, Violin, 1968-

Emilio was with John Mack and Bill Steck in Hartford at a restaurant with a revolving bar. "As you know, John didn't drink Coke so we all ordered cocktails, and who came into the non-moving part of the restaurant but Louis Lane and Szell. There we were turning around with our drinks; it was the afternoon of a concert — lunchtime. We tried every which way to cover our drinks as the thing rotated around to where they were sitting. It was one of those 'Oh, no,' moments. If he even saw you around the lobby at four in the afternoon he would say: 'why aren't you in your room taking a nap?' The afternoon nap was mandatory."

Emilio admired Szell's great respect for music. "He had no patience for mediocrity and would intimidate people because he was such a perfectionist. He knew every note of every score and he wanted it to be perfect. Thursday morning rehearsals were often the best performances of the week."

I recalled that Szell used to say: "We give nine concerts a week, seven of them in private." I then asked Emilio about his first rehearsal. "It was so perfect, so sculpted, the balance was like a jewel. The wind section was incredible. Everyone played in the same style. They all articulated the same way, all had the same musical intention, trademarks of the orchestra. They all played like one instrument. If one looks at Szell's scores in the library, every score is marked, string parts are all bowed meticulously."

Szell was always threatening to reduce the size of the string section if it didn't improve. At times he ran roughshod over some of the most magnificently talented people. But, as Emilio suggested, "something important was happening in Severance Hall. There was electricity in the air."

Emilio got a last minute call to audition for Cleveland. With only one week to prepare, he declined. "When I hung up, my wife asked who called and what I had said. When she heard my reply she said: 'Call him back.' I said: 'You call him back. I'm the one who has to play.' I called him back! That was 1968."

One of Emilio's most vivid memories was in Osaka, Japan on Szell's final tour. "When the last note of the last encore sounded there was a huge roar of approval from the audience, and even after the orchestra left the stage, people were lined up trying to touch his hand."

He also recalled a tape recording that he got from the local classical music station with two gems on it: "One, he was addressing a women's group and at the end of the remarks he thanked the women for the work they had done. He said: 'Thank you from my bottom to my heart.' The other was a tape of Gilels sitting at the piano with Szell at another piano. Szell, talking in German was actually coaching Gilels — giving Gilels a lesson!"

At one point Emilio thought of auditioning for the assistant concertmaster position, so he decided to ask Szell his opinion. "Szell was very complimentary and when I said: 'What should I do?' he replied: 'I cannot think of any more recognition than what I have given you in the last minute.' And that was the end of it."

"Do you remember," Emilio asked me, "Symon Goldberg, the famous violinist? He came to conduct and play. We were rehearsing a Mozart concerto when we noticed Szell lurking behind a pillar listening. Suddenly, there was Szell at the podium touching the score. Goldberg said: 'Is there anything wrong?' Szell said: 'That note! Incorrect!' Goldberg had brought his own score containing the printed error. Of course, our parts had been corrected. Szell was tough, but he put the orchestra on the map!"

Martin Flowerman, Double Bass, 1967-2011
Yarden Faden, Viola, 1966-2006

Yarden: Szell's office overlooked the parking lot. Every morning about 9 he watched to see who came early, what kind of car you drove, and whether or not you were carrying music. Ralph Schiller, a violinist, used to stand in front of Szell's closed office door playing his violin to make an impression. It backfired. One day Szell opened the door and said: "Ralph, I don't like the sound of your instrument." When Ralph explained that he couldn't afford a new violin right now, Szell responded: "Last week you drove up in a brand new Buick."

Marty: I remember the first speech I heard Szell give. It was the day the orchestra began rehearsing for the European Festival tour and he told us where to go for dinner in Salzburg. It was a place with plain, unadulterated meat without gravies and sauces so we wouldn't get sick. It was a place called the "Eulenspiegel" and it was really great.

Yarden: I was one of the few people who signed a contract without auditioning for Szell. Louis Lane hired me and at my first rehearsal Szell saw a stranger in the viola section. I can't remember if it was the Brahm's Academic Overture or the Tragic Overture. But it was always said that with Szell the "Academic" was very tragic and the "Tragic" was academic.

Szell couldn't get enough rehearsal time and Maazel couldn't wait to be finished. When Maazel first came we performed and recorded Prokofiev's "Romeo and Juliet." I couldn't believe the limited amount of rehearsal time and how Maazel accomplished it. He was the best technician I've ever played with.

Marty: Whenever Lane took over, he would conduct just like Szell. He was a quick study. Just before Szell's death, I was in line at the last breakfast before we left Sapporo for Seoul. Lane was in line looking very sad. He must have gotten word of Szell's condition. He was reminiscing about when he came to the orchestra and knew nothing about conducting. He is an incredible sight-reader.

Yarden: Charlie Trager had won the Tchaikovsky Competition in '62 or '63 and was starting a solo career. He was really self-taught and an incredible talent. He had the attitude that he knew what to do and he did it. He played a Mozart concerto many times on tour with us and at one point he changed everything, fingerings, everything. The next time he played it Szell said: "Tell me, with whom did you study Mozart?" Charlie got his hackles up and said: "There is more than one way to play Mozart." Szell said: "Not in my orchestra."

The Sixties: Three Festival Tour, Europe - 1967; Blossom Music Center

The eleven and a half week tour of 1965 to the Soviet Union and Europe placed the Cleveland's prestige at the very top of the world's orchestras. In 1967 an invitation to perform in Salzburg, Lucerne and Edinburgh became the frosting on the cake...the final validation, and it most certainly came at the invitation of Europe's "General Music Director," Herbert von Karajan. Karajan's celebrity status in Europe and his power and influence cannot be exaggerated. He had film star looks, a magnetic personality, and a beautiful actress wife. He drove fast, expensive cars and piloted his own jet plane. His every action was covered in the press with fevered approval. A master musician, he lived up to his reputation. In London an orchestra was created just for him to record, despite the fact that his recordings with the Berlin, the Vienna, La Scala Opera, just to name a few, filled the catalog. He didn't want a guest conducting tour of America, but he wanted to lead the Cleveland Orchestra.

After the endless Soviet and European journey a couple of years earlier, the world's three great Festival cities (with a short diversion to London for recording) in three weeks looked really good to the musicians. There would be time to rest, to sightsee and to practice. The audiences would be some of the most sophisticated in the world.

By the later sixties it was clear that the smallish big city by the lake had a tiger by the tail. George Szell had fulfilled his promise. In the eyes of the world, the orchestra was "Second to None." Well and good, but in the real world the Clevelanders were far behind others in the "big five." Applause and critical praise is one thing but then musicians like everyone else must support themselves and their families. Though opposed by their boss, concerned that an extended season would cause artistic "burnout" among the players, a fifty-two week season seemed the inevitable.

Prescient supporters saw the need for the orchestra to have a summer home in the countryside, convenient to concertgoers over all the region. Emily Blossom, charming and energetic, and the Blossom family, led the way with a generous gift. Funds were raised, land was purchased, a brilliant architect set to work, and a stunning outdoor concert space was created. A space where thousands of music lovers would share a natural setting. Where birds would sing to music of the masters.

Despite worries that his musicians' artistic souls would be depleted by so many concerts and rehearsals each year, Szell plunged into all aspects of the project finally leading unforgettable concerts in the new venue. Ugly, longstanding problems with the Union were softening toward solution.

William Slocum, Horn, 1966-1968

Bill recounted a time on tour in Philadelphia. "John Rautenberg, Tom Peterson and I went to Bookbinders for lunch. We had martinis and were having a wonderful time. Guess who came in? Szell, no entourage, all by himself. And, by god, they seated him at the table next to ours. That quickly changed the dynamics of our conversation. He smiled and greeted us in that charming way he had. But, of course, for us, that was it for fun. He ordered a big lobster and they brought it with the appropriate utensils. Believe me, even after several martinis we were most conscious that he was there. He started to eat the lobster and knocked the whole thing off the table, plate and all, crashing to the floor. We could barely keep straight faces. In fact, we couldn't. But Szell just made a simple gesture with his hand — well, you see what has happened — and all with total decorum. It was simply sheer terror that kept us from breaking up completely."

Bill came to the orchestra after the Soviet Union tour but was on the 1967 tour, which he found to be incredible. "There was never an empty seat in the hall. As an encore, we played the 'Slavonic Dances' of Dvorak. When the concert ended, the audience applauded for ten or fifteen minutes. It was just so unbelievably beautiful."

Bill recalled the time pianist Clifford Curzon was rehearsing the "Emperor Concerto" in Cleveland. "He played all those cadenzas and during one, he got tied up in knots. Curzon didn't like to fly and had taken an all night train to Cleveland. Szell turned to him in a sharp voice and said: 'If you had flown, that probably wouldn't have happened.'"

160

Slocum was there for a curious performance when Oistrach played the Brahms Violin Concerto, then led the Shostakovich Tenth Symphony from the podium. Oistrach's conducting far from matched his violin playing. After a time there was a moment of chaos when half the orchestra separated from the other half by a measure or more. "The orchestra was so used to having nothing go wrong. Sometimes after the concerts I'd go out with Bob Marcellus and Tom Peterson. We'd go to one of the local bars with peanut shucks all over the floor and have a boilermaker. That night we went to the bar, ordered our boilermakers — a shot and a beer. We drank and none of us said anything. Then we ordered another boilermaker. After three of them, Marcellus turned to me and said: 'What happened?' I don't think anybody knew."

Bill, a conductor now, told me he often thinks of Szell's solutions to performance problems in the standard repertoire because Szell knew so many ways of solving them. "Going to Cleveland changed my whole life," Bill shared with me. "There were many times Bob Marcellus and I listened to music all night long. He had a marvelous record collection and intense love of music. All of that was part of an era. I felt like something special and magical was happening. I am sorry I didn't get to work with Marc Lifschey. I have his recordings, speaking of extraordinary, and always wonder how anybody could do what he did. I noticed by the time I was in the orchestra that each time we got to the place in the Prokofiev Fifth where the 'incident' happened, something weird happened to the orchestra.

I asked Bill whether he thought this anecdotal history of the era was an important thing to do. "Yes, I do. How many orchestras had such great artists? Weeks could go by and you would never hear an out of tune woodwind chord. Szell would get things to an incredible place where others could not go. He would say: 'Do you believe it?' He was right to say that. You've got to believe it."

John Mack, Oboe, 1965-2001
David Zauder, Trumpet, 1958-1997

Larry: Well, well, here's the "late" Mr. Personnel Manager!

David: Yes, and somewhere in the world it's happy hour. I'll take bourbon!

Larry: So tell us about your experience with Szell.

David: I can't say he was the Second Coming but he knew I was able to play how and what he wished. He selected the place, the time, the person, the instrument, the style. I learned to understand his philosophy.

John: Tell us about the low e flat!

David: Well, that was part of his major strategy. He was in his office before nine and saw everybody park and walk in. Obviously he saw me. I went to Case Western Reserve University for a class from 7:30 to 8:30 a.m. At 8:45 I would walk into the hall with books in hand. So Szell called in Trogdon, the personnel manager, and said: "What is that kid doing? I see him here at a quarter to nine and he has **books**!"

Trogdon called me in and asked what I was doing. I told him I was going to business school. Next thing I know Szell tells me he doesn't trust me to play the e flat in the Schumann "Manfred" Overture. I played it perfectly Monday, Tuesday, Wednesday and Thursday in rehearsal, and at the concert, and at the Friday recording. But Saturday night the low e flat didn't speak. Remember this is February, 1960. I got a pink slip from Barksdale, A. Beverly Barksdale, the general manager. It said: Your contract is ending. You will not be reengaged. "What are you talking about," I asked him and he told me to talk to the "boss." So I did!

"You know," said Szell, "In November, we did the whole Schumann cycle. The low e flat didn't speak out on Saturday night." I asked what he meant. I had no clue. True, we played the whole week of Schumann and recorded it on Friday, but there is no e flat on the b flat trumpet, only e natural so I said: 'Maestro, you hired me to play. I am a trumpet player and you are asking me to play notes that are not on the instrument. I don't think that is fair. I don't have the mouthpiece to play low e flat but I was very lucky to play it six times in a row.' He said: 'Okay, I will extend your contract for '60-'61 if you agree to be Trogdon's assistant and help him with the five-week tour to the west coast. Quickly I accepted. I was in charge of train and bus arrangements. At any rate, those were his conditions and in fact it wasn't about the one note that didn't speak on Saturday night. It was his way of getting me involved as Trogdon's assistant.

Of course, after that it took four years. I played auditions for four years with different instruments and different mouthpieces until he accepted the sound I produced. I went to the factory almost every year to have work done on my instrument until 1964 just before we went to Carnegie Hall to play the Beethoven Ninth. It was the same weekend the Beatles arrived in New York. He finally agreed that I had the right instrument, the right mouthpiece, and the right quality sound.

After that we did a lot of recording. He controlled every note we played. It wasn't something that you just

164

put out there. I don't think there was any other conductor who paid attention to the fifth horn, the third trumpet or the second bassoon in order to achieve the kind of sound and balance he was looking for. Every three months I would go in and play an audition. I auditioned for six years. I didn't get tenure for **six** years.

John: He affected us so deeply that the orchestra has survived to this day with a strong sense of duty toward the music. It was lodged in the musicians and passed on.

Larry: When I retired in 1995 I was quoted in the newspaper as saying: "It's still George Szell's orchestra."

David: In today's arena of contractual obligations, trade agreements and limitations — his dominance of players' time and performance would not be tolerated. He told you what instrument to play, what mouthpiece to play and how to do it. Today there is none of that. There are limitations as to responsibility and areas of influence. The problem is that the people today cannot or do not trust the leadership. That was not the case with Szell. You trusted, you knew. He couldn't conduct a complex rhythm but you knew damn well that the music you played and how you played it was absolutely honest.

I want to tell you about one incident that happened towards the end. It was 1968. We had a committee meeting during which Elmer Setzer said to Szell: "You have to get behind us and help us get financial security, year-round employment." Szell said to Elmer: "If you insist on a fifty-two week season count me **out**! There is no musician who should be asked to even think about playing significant orchestral music fifty-two weeks a year. It just cannot be done."

Larry: John, what was your audition like?

John: The first time was during the Casals Festival in the south of France. A friend told me Szell was coming to hear me play. I didn't believe it but the next morning in rehearsal I looked out front and said to myself: 'Oh, my god, there's a skull out there that's easily recognizable.' At a break Szell came to me and asked me to play for him the next day. 'Yes, where?' I asked. 'Right here,' he replied. This was an abbey that was having its 100th anniversary. Its floor was gravel and someone was painting the stage. So when tomorrow came, the tone sounded about the size of the head of a pin. I played for him for 35 minutes. He then turned, heels crunching in the gravel and said: 'That's all I want to hear. Thank you very much.'

At my next audition I played for Szell for an hour and twenty minutes. They don't do that these days. The last piece was the Bartok Concerto for Orchestra which I had never played. He pointed to the fourth movement and I fumbled my way through it. The third time I played for him, the orchestra was in Washington, D.C. and Marc was out of the orchestra. This time I only played for half an hour. It was a formality. He said: "Mr. Mack, would you please play a D major scale slowly up two octaves and down", which I did. He said: "How curious. While I might find your high A quite satisfactory on the way down, I find it decidedly flat on the way up." So I had to play my high A's too high for about two and a half years.

David: Szell was very short on appreciation, compliments and the ability to empathize. He often didn't appreciate what people were going through. Consequently he made us feel that he was an SOB — that we sweated our bones for him and he didn't even care.

In 1968 we recorded the Prokofiev "Lieutenant Kije Suite." I played the cornet part. The cornet plays a solo off stage in the first and fourth movements and is joined at the end by the violas. I was hyperventilating but I played the opening nine times and it was always the same. He never said a word. We finished, went to the last movement and he turned to Abe who later told me: "That's the way I always felt a cornet should sound." That was his compliment to me via Abe. After ten years of sweating for the man! He expected it as a matter of course. He was not very appreciative of individual effort. He felt it was your duty. Sometimes he could be loyal and involved, however.

Larry: I remember when Don White came to the orchestra and we went on a southern tour. Everyone was concerned there could be racial events. We developed a petition which we all signed saying that if there was any difficulty because of Don, the orchestra would refuse to play wherever that happened. It was sent to the management and Szell signed it himself.

David: You were there in '58 in North Carolina when they wouldn't let Don in the hotel because he was black. Szell told them: "If he doesn't stay with us, we don't play, we leave."

John: To Szell, the Mozart piano concerti were the finest flowers of musical art. And when Szell did them, they were filled with mystery.

Larry: How long were you with Szell?

John: Five years with George Szell, no, ten years, ten years. One year with Szell counts for two years.

Larry: I think of him every day. I remember how we rehearsed the Beethoven symphonies over and over. During a rehearsal at Smith College we were about to do the "Eroica" and I saw on his face what I thought was worry, almost fear. I interpreted it this way: he was almost praying that he would be able to do justice to this music. I think that is what drove him. I don't think he thought anyone else could do justice to the music. Therefore the responsibility was his alone.

David: Were you in his office in Anchorage before the last concert we played with him?

John: I spoke to him on stage.

David: Bob Marcellus, Mike Bloom and I were in his office just before the concert. I don't know who else. He said: "Please don't expect from me what I've always been able to give you. Do what you know is right and good luck." He barely got through that program.

John: About a half year ago I heard a rebroadcast of something we did in Boston. It was honed to perfection and everything sounded so spiffy.

Larry: He could handle a slow tempo. He held the pace but the music always moved forward. I know contracts and salaries were at Szell's discretion. What experience did you have with that?

David: My first contract was below what I was making playing "My Fair Lady." I said: "I can't take the job." He said: "Okay, Okay. I'll give you another five dollars. I want you here. Now you go home and learn how to play pianissimo." I was making $148.50 playing seven shows a week. He offered me $115 and finally $120. I thought I should give it a shot.

The principals often had to go to his home to perform. These events were lessons, of course, where they came under even closer scrutiny. If I had a dollar for every time a principal player did this, I'd be living in the Bahamas now.

He was in a perfect zone with other performance-oriented entities. For instance, the Cleveland Browns had Paul Brown, the Packers had Lombardi. These people were giants because they got their players to perform in a manner to achieve ultimate success. Consequently, those who could not cope were not happy and didn't last. But the fact remains that those who established the reputation of this orchestra were those who complied with the man's idiosyncrasies.

My objective was to play like Harry James and marry Betty Grable. I subjugated myself to play for George Szell who never, **never** said "Nice job."

Touring Japan, Korea and Alaska – 1970

The Cleveland Orchestra's final tour with Szell took us to the Far East for the first time. It was a fascinating discovery of a new audience, an interaction of cultures, old and new, Eastern, American and European. The Japanese were wonderful hosts, doing their best to make things go smoothly, solving every problem. Patrons were so attentive as to be almost unreal. Mixed with an intense courtesy was an amazing energy, an electricity in the concert hall. There was never a cough, never a dropped program booklet. The orchestra was in its prime, concerts and their reception were breathtaking. Szell had mellowed noticeably, taking pleasure in the instrument he and we had built. Clearly more relaxed than in the rugged past, he continued to lead his orchestra with precision and unquestionable taste.

Among the musicians on this tour was the new cellist Michael Haber.

Michael Haber, Cello, 1969-1971

Michael was very reluctant to be interviewed. He protested that he was the "last and the least person" I should ask. His stories might be amusing but he wasn't sure they should be published because they would not reflect well on George Szell. I assured him I wanted to show Szell as a human being, flaws and all.

"He was a jerk...to people like me," Michael began. "I think Szell's mind worked in a hierarchical manner. A soloist or principal would find him to be brilliant, charming, deeply educated, the sophisticated person that he undoubtedly was. But if you were an insignificant person...you know the orchestra didn't sound any different if I showed up for the concert...he knew that perfectly well. He needed me to sit there but I never got to see the whole man. That is why comments from me are not pertinent."

I tried to calm Michael and explain to him that what he had said was true for all of us and that we wanted a complete picture of Szell, the man. Speaking of pictures, we had just acquired several pictures of Mr. Szell that had not often been on display. I showed them to Michael and he acknowledged them but seemed eager to share with me how Szell had made him feel and put an end to this uncomfortable encounter with the past.

"I was terribly intimidated by him at first. But when I realized that he was not the kind of man that ultimately I admire, when I saw him behave in ways that seemed like a small human being with a smaller wing span, then I lost my fear of him. He was a great musician but that was not enough for me...some of his pettiness, over controlling, refusing to engage me...little old me, twenty-six years old, a nobody...for his refusal to engage me as a legitimate human being, I despised him. I absolutely despised him."

I must admit I found Michael's declaration refreshing in a way because I had done so many interviews of people who spoke of Szell as if he were a kindly sort of grandfather. As I mentioned this to Michael he quickly interrupted me...

"Let me talk!! You are the biggest blabberer but I love every word of it." Michael, now in a philosophical tone..."I just need to explain something about myself. I take a very dim view of my opinions. The older I get, the more ignorant I realize I am. I personally think that is a sign of intelligence but most people would not."

"Ignorance, a sign of intelligence?" I asked.

"No, the sense of your own ignorance is a sign of intelligence. A sense of somebody else's ignorance is a sign of cruelty."

With that philosophical discussion concluded, Michael was able to venture into a description of his audition with the orchestra. Michael had started out as an amateur musician four and a half years before he came to his first orchestra audition. He was in the Army band in Washington, D.C. when he came to Cleveland for an audition. While waiting to be called, another cellist came downstairs saying: "He made me begin 'Don Juan' with a down bow." Michael replied that he could hardly play it starting up bow OR down bow. When Michael's turn came, with little hope and much trepidation he went on stage, hoping not to make a fool of himself before Szell. "If you were a music lover which basically was all I was at that point...George Szell and the Cleveland Orchestra, I mean that was IT. So I played a movement of a

172

concerto and a whole movement of a Bach suite. Lynn Harrell came on stage while I played some difficult cello passages from the Beethoven Eighth Symphony. When I finished, Lynn said to me: 'use a long stroke' and Szell yelled from the back of the hall: "**Lynn, this isn't a cello lesson!**" I was very grateful. I played it again and played it better.

"We had to fill out a questionnaire prior to the audition listing our previous experience. All I could write was United States Army Band. 'Mr. Haber,' Szell said, 'is that really your only experience?' Michael had to admit that was correct. So for the remainder of the audition, Szell stood next to him and had him repeat two very difficult cello passages from "Don Juan" four or five times. Then he put on the stand an obscure passage from the Brahms Second Symphony. "Finally I was finished and satisfied that I had played well but knew that I could never do it again!" Szell offered him the job 'if you want to come and learn.'

Michael was soon to find life working for Szell a bit difficult. He confided that "Szell struck me as a repressed, self-contained man with little social grace toward peons like me." Michael was very nervous playing his first rehearsal. One of the pieces was the Bartered Bride Overture. "There I was playing a piece I was frightened of, with a man I was terrified of, and I must have looked so scared that Teddy Barr reached out and patted my knee. It was very sweet of him." I recalled how Teddy Barr and Albert Michelson sat together in an uncomfortable truce. Michelson always demanded more room for himself with the result that Teddy had a hard time seeing the music on their shared music stand. One time, Albert, a Russian émigré, said to Teddy: "We must fight" as if he were challenging him to a duel with ancient pistols. Michael conjectured that more than half the orchestra at that time were refugees. "If you get a bunch of mostly European refugees with tortured, complicated pasts and put them together, it is a gallery, not that everybody is necessarily pleasant or that you want to be friends with all of them, but these are human beings who have really lived."

Michael's favorite music beyond all other was Haydn and Mozart and the orchestra was famous for playing these composers. However, there was no rotation so only the first few players in the section had the opportunity to play this music. One day Michael was able to get an appointment to talk to Szell. When he walked into Szell's office, Szell's immediate reaction was to ask: "**What's Wrong?**" He was ready for a complaint. However, Michael said: "There's nothing wrong, Mr. Szell" which shocked Szell and caused him to retreat behind his desk awaiting Michael's explanation. Michael explained that Haydn and Mozart are his favorite composers, he loved the way Szell and the orchestra played their music, and he would like the opportunity to participate. Szell told Michael that he was thinking of doing some sort of rotation in the future. "Of course, the following season he died but from that point on when he realized that I had just come with a request from my heart as an artist, he was very nice.

"Since we are talking, I would like to say one thing about the music making. Again it is a point of view of someone who is twenty-six. But when we played a Beethoven symphony, a Brahms, a Schubert, a Bruckner or a Mahler symphony with Szell, those evenings were absolutely unforgettable for me. I felt a real depth of

174

understanding and that something very special was happening. There were a lot of other concerts where his deep need to control everything spoiled things for me. But there were five or six or seven or eight evenings during my first year in the orchestra that represented, even to my memory now, full justification for my having wanted to become a musician. They were that special."

Final Chapter - 1970

The day of the last concert in Alaska I caused Szell a bit of consternation. I had recently gotten my pilot's license and had taken Louis Lane and Joseph Adato for a ride around the Anchorage area. Szell heard about it and when he saw me entering the hall before the concert said: "You drove that airplane all around the airport, took it up, up in the air — and you took **Louis!!** — and you brought him back safe and sound." I said: "Yes," Mr. Szell, it was very important for me to bring Louis back safely. "Why's that? Why's that?" he demanded. "So that I could come back safely, Mr. Szell." His response was like the sound of an old car starting up... "**Har, Har**" Then he wanted to know all about my piloting. "How long have you been flying?" I thought: I can't tell him the truth. He'd be really upset. Desperate, I began to think of "stories" and tried to create a fantasy personal history. I knew what he was thinking... "I'm 73 years old and I've never flown in a small plane. Louis has done it now. I can't understand how Larry learned to fly. He's a bass player and shouldn't be doing anything else. Still perhaps I should ask him to take me up for a ride!" And I kept thinking...**What** am I going to tell him? Finally I came to grips with the inevitable reality, I absolutely could not lie to him. When again the question came up "How long have you had your license?" I choked out: "I've had my license for nine months, Mr. Szell. Till then he had looked like the Commendatore, the imposing stone statue in "Don Giovanni." Well, you should have seen that stone crackling right down to the stage floor.

During the orchestra's final concert he seemed to look over at me from time to time, still surprised that I could fly. But what I noticed even more were the subtle moments when his baton seemed to falter. He looked so very tired. In Soporo, northern Japan doctors strongly advised him not to conduct the next concerts but he felt obligated to the audiences in Korea and Alaska.

Szell in Tokyo

The flight from Seoul to Anchorage had been unusually long. There were delays and fuel problems brought on by bad airline planning. For everyone the trip was energy depleting, exhausting. But once in our places, warmed up, ready to accept his musical challenges, we settled in for what would be our final curtain call with the magnificent giant who had brought us so far and taught us so much.

A Rare Moment

Index

- Alfred Genovese - Oboe, 1959-1960
- Michael Grebanier - Cello, 1959-1963
- Arnold Steinhardt - Violin, 1959-1964
- **Touring the Soviet Union – 1965**
- **Yuri - Who Is This Guy?**
- Dialogue:
    - Diane Mather - Cello, 1963-2001
    - Robert Perry - Cello, 1968-1994
    - John Rautenberg - Flute, 1961-2005
    - Muriel Carmen - Viola, 1951-1994
- Theodore Johnson -Clarinet, 1959-1995
- Jerry Rosen - Violin, 1959-1967
- Michael Goldman - Violin, 1962-1965; 1969-1973
- Allen Kofsky - Trombone, 1961-2000
- Elmer & Marie Setzer:
    - Elmer Setzer - Violin, 1949-1990
    - Marie Setzer - Violin, 1961-1990
- Richard Wiener - Percussion, 1963-2013
- Bernard Adelstein - Trumpet, 1960-1988
- Lynn Harrell - Cello, 1963-1970
- Jorge Sicre - Cello, 1961-1991
- Thomas Wohlwender - Trumpet, 1960-1971
- Dialogue:
    - Gary Tischkoff - Violin, 1966-2009
    - Felix Kraus - Oboe, English Horn, 1963-2004
    - Alvaro DeGranda - Violin, 1966-2006
- Dialogue:
    - Bert Siegel - Violin, 1965-1995
    - Joan Siegel - Violin, 1965-1995
    - Ed Ormond - Viola, 1959-1997
- Emilio Llinas - Violin, 1968-
- Dialogue:
    - Martin Flowerman - Double Bass, 1967-2011
    - Yarden Faden - Viola, 1966-2006
- **The Sixties: Three Festival Tour, Europe - 1967; Blossom Music Center**
- William Slocum - Horn, 1966-1968

About the Authors

Lawrence Angell
Larry retired as Principal Double Bass in 1995 after 40 years working for the Cleveland Orchestra - 15 of those under George Szell. His is married to the outstanding pianist Anita Pontremoli. Larry is licensed pilot and flight instructor.

Bernette Jaffe
Bernette Jaffe has her PhD in Education and spent her working career as head of the Ratner Schools. Her three sons and daughter in laws are her pride and joy as well as her eight grandchildren.

About the Book

One of the greatest conductors of the 20th century, George Szell led the Cleveland Orchestra from 1946 until his death in 1970. A meticulous perfectionist, Szell was known to be an autocratic taskmaster who wielded total artistic control. Under his leadership he transformed the orchestra into a world class ensemble. **Tales From the Locker Room** gives a rare, honest, humorous and at times brutal look at this musical genius through first hand interviews, stories, and anecdotes by members of the Cleveland Orchestra who served under him.